Tropical Fish
for Community Tanks

By Waltraud Weiss

Translated by
U. ERICH FRIESE
Animal Facilities
University of New South Wales
Sydney, Australia

t.f.h.

ISBN 0-86622-102-6

Originally published in German by Franckh'sche Verlagshandlung, W. Keller & Co., Stuttgart/1980 under the title *Fische furs Gesellscahaftsbecken.*

Photos by: Dr. H. R. Axelrod (9); H. Bleher (1); J. Elias (1); S. Frank (1); M. Gilroy (2); Dr. H. Grier (2); B. Kahl (51); A. Norman (1); W. Paccagnella (1); K. Paysan (1); S. Pecolatto (1); H. J. Richter (19); A. Roth (4); W. Tomey (1); A. van den Nieuwenhuizen (1); B. Walker (1); K. Zahradka (1); and R. Zukal (4).

Front cover: a pair of black ruby barbs, male below; photo by H.J. Richter. **Back cover:** red wagtail platies; photo by Kremser. **Title page:** red platies; photo by R. Zukal.

Distributed in the UNITED STATES by T.F.H. Publications, Inc., 211 West Sylvania Avenue, Neptune City, NJ 07753; in CANADA by H & L Pet Supplies Inc., 27 Kingston Crescent, Kitchener, Ontario N2B 2T6; Rolf C. Hagen Ltd., 3225 Sartelon Street, Montreal 382 Quebec; in ENGLAND by T.F.H. Publications Limited, 4 Kier Park, Ascot, Berkshire SL5 7DS; in AUSTRALIA AND THE SOUTH PACIFIC by T.F.H. (Australia) Pty. Ltd., Box 149, Brookvale 2100 N.S.W., Australia; in NEW ZEALAND by Ross Haines & Son, Ltd., 18 Monmouth Street, Grey Lynn, Auckland 2 New Zealand; in SINGAPORE AND MALAYSIA by MPH Distributors (S) Pte., Ltd., 601 Sims Drive, # 03/07/21, Singapore 1438; in the PHILIPPINES by Bio-Research, 5 Lippay Street, San Lorenzo Village, Makati Rizal; in SOUTH AFRICA by Multipet Pty. Ltd., 30 Turners Avenue, Durban 4001. Published by T.F.H. Publications Inc. Manufactured in the United States of America by T.F.H. Publications, Inc.

INTRODUCTION 4

THE COMMUNITY AQUARIUM 10

BOTTOM FISHES 16

Corydoras aeneus - 16; *Corydoras paleatus* - 18; *Hoplosternum thoracatum* - 20; *Pseudocrenilabrus multicolor* - 22; *Pelvicachromis pulcher* - 24; *Hemichromis thomasi* - 26; *Apistogramma borelli* - 28; *Nannacara anomala* - 30; *Acanthophthalmus kuhlii* - 32; *Acanthophthalmus semicinctus* - 36; *Botia macracantha* - 36; *Botia sidthimunki* - 38; *Labeo bicolor* - 40; *Gyrinocheilus aymonieri* - 42

SCHOOLING FISHES ABOVE THE BOTTOM 44

Melanotaenia maccullochi - 44; *Hemigrammus erythrozonus* -46; *Paracheirodon innesi* - 48; *Paracheirodon axelrodi* - 50; *Puntius conchonius* - 52; *Puntius nigrofasciatus* - 54; *Capoeta oligolepis* -56; *Capoeta "schuberti"* - 58; *Capoeta tetrazona* - 60; *Capoeta titteya* - 62

MID-WATER SCHOOLING FISHES 62

Aphyocharax anisitsi - 62; *Ctenobrycon spilurus* - 64; *Gymnocorymbus ternetzi* - 66; *Hemigrammus caudovittatus* - 68; *Hasemania nana* - 70; *Hemigrammus ocellifer* - 70; *Hyphessobrycon callistus* - 72; *Hyphessobrycon flammeus* - 74; *Hyphessobrycon bentosi* - 76; *Hyphessobrycon pulchripinnis* - 78; *Hyphessobrycon erythrostigma* - 80; *Pristella maxillaris* - 80; *Phenacogrammus interruptus* - 82; *Tanichthys albonubes* - 84

MID-WATER FISHES, DENSELY PLANTED 86

Colisa fasciata - 86; *Colisa lalia* - 88; *Trichogaster leeri* - 90; *Trichogaster trichopterus* - 92; *Helostoma temmincki* - 94; *Pterophyllum scalare* - 96

SCHOOLING FISHES OF UPPER WATERS 98

Gasteropelecus sternicla - 98; *Thayeria boehlkei* - 100; *Brachydanio albolineatus* - 102; *Brachydanio frankei* - 104; *Brachydanio nigrofasciatus* - 106; *Brachydanio rerio* - 108; *Rasbora dorsiocellata* - 110; *Rasbora heteromorpha* - 112; *Rasbora trilineata* - 114

LIVEBEARERS OF THE UPPER WATERS 116

Poecilia reticulata - 116; *Poecilia velifera* - 118; *Poecilia* sp. -120; *Xiphophorus helleri* - 122; *Xiphophorus helleri* X *Xiphophorus maculatus* - 124; *Xiphophorus maculatus* - 125; *Xiphophorus variatus* - 125

INTRODUCTION

What are the species of fishes that are compatible in a community aquarium? From among the hundreds that could have been selected, only 60 were chosen for discussion in this book. These are the ones that have been favorites with aquarists for many years and are commonly available from petshops. Most of the fishes selected are very colorful, and some also display a particularly interesting type of behavior. All are generally peaceful, are easily kept, and do not require special attention to water conditions.

All species chosen do well in soft to medium-hard water of about 15° German hardness (°dH). To give you some idea of how the dH scale works, 3° dH is considered very soft and 8° to 15° dH is medium-hard. You can find the average hardness of your local water by testing it with kits available at your petshop or sometimes by asking your local water supply agency or water department. It should be kept in mind that details about water chemistry are really important only when fish breeding is being contemplated. A community or mixed display tank rarely permits successful fish breeding.

Temperature Charts

Throughout this book representations of thermometer readings accompany sections of text dealing with the different species discussed; figures given in these illustrations are in Centigrade degrees. Readers who find it more convenient to do their aquarium maintenance figurings in terms of Fahrenheit readings rather than Centigrade readings can use the approximating Fahrenheit equivalents shown here.

°C.	=	°F.
30	=	86
29	=	84
28	=	82
27	=	81
26	=	79
25	=	77
24	=	75
23	=	73
22	=	72
21	=	70
20	=	68
19	=	66

Keeping tropical fishes can be a simple, relaxing hobby if you choose the right fishes to begin with. Some of the most simple fishes to keep are also among the most colorful—and many species can be bred by even a complete beginner.

Certain fishes indicate by their body shape what is their preferred habitat. Some species prefer to remain close to the bottom (clown loaches, catfishes): others stay in the middle region of the tank (barbs and related fishes); and others always stay close to the surface (hatchetfishes). The bottom-dwellers are often elongated or eel-like in shape or have a flattened abdominal area (belly). A streamlined or torpedo-like shape is indicative of a fast-swimming fish in the open middle regions of the tank. Those species found at the surface almost invariably have a straight dorsal profile and may possess a keel-like abdomen.

Such generalized groupings of fishes according to their habitat (remembering that there are exceptions and transitional forms) should enable you to select your fishes in such a way that they are indeed compatible and so that all zones or regions in your tank are actually populated.

There is no general rule-of-thumb for the maximum number of fishes that can be kept in a tank. This is very much dependent upon the size of the fish, their level of activity, and also upon the effectiveness of the filter.

It is advisable to concentrate on a few selected groups of fishes rather than "cramming" the tank indiscriminately with all sorts of species. Typical schooling fish such as barbs must never be kept as individuals, otherwise they will lose their colors and their activity will diminish; some may even become aggressive toward other tank inhabitants. There should be at least six individuals of each schooling species, preferably a dozen, which should all be bought at the same time to assure compatibility. The temperature scale shown alongside each species description is based on personal observations supplemented with information from

The common aquarium fishes can be readily divided into just a few groupings by their behavior in the aquarium—some fishes school, others are solitary; some never leave the surface; some stay on the bottom and will not rise to the surface even to feed; others range over much of the aquarium in large or small groups. To keep fishes successfully you must remember their position in the ecology of the aquarium.

The zebra danio, *Brachydanio rerio,* is one of many inexpensive, readily available, and hardy fishes found in almost any pet shop all year 'round.

literature. If fish are kept at the indicated optimum temperature (the darkest area of the scale) there should really be no problems. The adjacent values (lighter shade) indicate the temperature latitude accepted by a particular species. This is important for trying to keep species with slightly different temperature requirements in the same aquarium. However, the listed tolerance should not be exceeded. Admittedly, many species are sufficiently robust to tolerate colder or warmer water – at least temporarily – but why tempt fate?

Pet store managers often speak of "bread and butter" fishes, the species and cultivated varieties that are the most commonly sold and form the backbone of the aquarium business. Always on the bread and butter list are the five major species of livebearers—the guppy, the swordtail, the two platies, and the black molly.

THE COMMUNITY AQUARIUM

The most popular type of aquarium is the general display or community tank where fishes are kept purely for esthetic reasons without consideration of their geographical origin or natural distribution. The only things that matter are that the fishes are compatible, that they have the same ecological requirements (food, temperature), and that the tank is set up in such a way as to provide satisfactory accommodation for all the species. Although some fishes survive under less than optimum conditions, it should be the objective of all aquarists to provide an environment in which the fishes can display the entire natural range of their normal activities.

Habitat fanatics among aquarists insist on correctly and scientifically landscaped aquarium. However, even an aquarium set up in great detail according to carefully researched ecological information or actual habitat studies does not provide the same conditions as found in nature. Water values available for a particular natural habitat are

Planted aquaria always add flair to the hobby. German and other Continental hobbyists always use living plants and consider plastic plants an abomination, but American aquarists are much more liberal in their use of artificials. The fishes really don't know the difference if they use the plants only as background and to lay their eggs on the leaves.

invariably only individual random condition measurements that have no relevance to seasonal variations in water quality normally found in a particular body of water.

The geographical distributions of some species, especially those from inaccessible tropical regions, are not always completely known. For instance, in one area a particular fish may be the dominant species, *i.e.*, it is characteristic for that area. Yet in another area the same species may be found only rarely, possibly due to inadvertent introductions of egg or larvae. Moreover, in heavy plant thickets and similar habitats that are hard to collect not all the species that occur may actually be found. Those fishes that are hard to catch in the wild may never find their way into an aquarium.

It is not advisable to try to duplicate the bottom of a rain forest stream by placing decaying leaves on the aquarium bottom; clean peat moss is far more effective. However, it is suggested that the subject of using peat moss in an aquarium be studied in some detail *before* it is actually placed in the tank. There is considerable danger in trying to do too much! It is far simpler for a beginning aquarist who wants to "improve" the water quality in his tank to use commercially available peat extracts and then carefully follow the instructions provided.

While the rainy season in the tropics is the growth period—the period of reproduction—many tropical fishes have by now adjusted their reproductive cycle to the "unnatural" conditions found in captivity. After all, food is always available in sufficient quantities. With a few tricks aquarists can also change water conditions in order to stimulate breeding several times throughout the year.

American aquarists are not too choosy about trying to duplicate a fish's natural habitat in miniature, but there are instances when a habitat must be at least partially duplicated. Fishes from dark, soft, acid waters (bottom) usually can be kept best in such waters, while fishes from the very hard, alkaline waters of the African Great Lakes (top) seldom survive in other types of water.

12

Most tropical fishes available through commercial channels are bred in local or overseas fish hatcheries. However, there are also quite a few species that are quite difficult to breed or that have never reproduced in captivity. Such wild-caught imported fishes are understandably expensive.

Although we have seen that setting up in our aquaria a genuine Southeast Asian rice paddy or a South American rain forest is essentially impossible, it can still be a lot of fun trying to approximate natural habitats. Alternatively, setting up a tank with fishes from only one continent or with representatives from only one family or genus (such as all gouramis or all livebearers) can also bring great pleasure.

A community tank must have a volume of at least 15 to 25 gallons. Smaller tanks can hold only a few species and their care is correspondingly more difficult as the water becomes dirtier quicker and temperature and water chemistry fluctuate faster. On the other hand, a large tank permits the fish to establish different territories. Controlled lighting can be arranged over different types of gravel or sand bottoms, permitting each group of fishes to have access to light and shade as it wishes.

It is best to determine the fish population for a particular community aquarium with a checklist at hand. Let us suppose you want to have a school of neon tetras. You record all important data (the main criterion is water temperature) and write down which other species are compatible with neons, what size your tank should be, what is required for setting up the tank, and which plants are suitable.

Finally, a small hint: Record your observations and experiences in a notebook—you will enjoy your hobby even more.

By doing a little background work in the literature you can prevent some problems before they happen. Before you buy that school of neon tetras, for instance, you should be aware of their preference for soft, acid water, the necessity to keep them in schools, and the fact that almost any larger fishes would consider them as food regardless of their bright colors.

14

BOTTOM FISHES
Family Callichthyidae

(South America: muddy bottoms)
Corydoras aeneus — Aeneus Catfish, Bronze Corydoras

°C

30
29
28
27
26
25
24
23
22
21
20
19

This species occurs in Trinidad, Venezuela, Guyana, Bolivia, Brazil, and the La Plata States—in other words, most of northern South America. It inhabits shallow areas in running and standing waters with soft bottoms. It even tolerates polluted water because in addition to the gills it has the ability to swallow atmospheric oxygen directly from the air at the water surface and absorb the oxygen through the walls of the intestine. This biological peculiarity has to be taken into consideration when buying the tank; it should be sufficiently large but not very high, so that the fish can easily reach the surface. Although *C. aeneus* can tolerate polluted water, the tank water should be filtered and look clear.

C. aeneus requires subdued lighting and an area along the bottom with soft substrate where it can "dig" (fine sand

Many species of corydoras catfishes are available in your pet shop. Unfortunately, many—or even most—are not identified as to species. Since almost all corydoras catfishes are similar in their behavior and requirements in the aquarium, they make equallly nice additions to the aquarium. The fish shown has been rather doubtfully identified as *Corydoras reticulatus*.

about an inch deep will do). If the remainder of the bottom is covered with gravel, care must be taken that the individual grains are not sharp—the taste-bud-equipped barbels are delicate and easily damaged. There should also be some hiding places such as roots or caves.

The maximum size of the aeneus catfish is a bit under 3 inches. It likes to be in the company of its own kind, so there should always be a group of them, the actual number depending very much on the size of the tank and the filtration capacity. These constantly "digging" fish can easily make a tank cloudy. However, an ample and frequent food supply tends to inhibit some of the digging activity. The food (dry taken but live preferred) should be dropped onto the bottom—these catfish can cleverly extract each and every little worm (bloodworms and tubifex are favorites) from among the sand or gravel grains. Moreover, *C. aeneus* and many other catfishes will also clean up all other left-over food in the tank. Aquarists have come up with many colloquial terms to describe the cleaning and scavenging activities of this little fish. It is hardy and adaptable and thus ideally suited for any community tank. For esthetic reasons it is preferably kept in the company of South American tetras.

Corydoras paleatus — Peppered Corydoras

This species has never been found in northern South America; instead, it is confined to southern Brazil and the La Plata area (Uruguay, Paraguay, northern Argentina). The peppered corydoras differs from *C. aeneus* most obviously in coloration and has been an aquarium fish for far longer than the bronze corydoras. It is alleged that the

°C

| 30 |
| 29 |
| 28 |
| 27 |
| 26 |
| 25 |
| 24 |
| 23 |
| 22 |
| 21 |
| 20 |
| 19 |

Top: *Corydoras aeneus,* The aeneus or bronze corydoras. This is one of the most familiar corydoras catfishes on the American market, and it is almost always available. **Bottom:** The peppered corydoras, *C. paleatus.* This interesting species, although not uncommon in the U.S., is more familiar to Continental hobbyists. An albino variety is often available.

18

famous Parisian fish expert Carbonnier actually bred *C. paleatus* as early as 1878. This species is also known to spawn in community tanks occasionally.

Males can be distinguished from females by their finnage; the male's dorsal fin is higher and more pointed than the female's, and the body is more slender than that of the female.

This long-lived species (a longevity of up to 12 years has been reported) has many fans among aquarists, so they often set up a corydoras tank in order to observe the peppered corydoras and several other species at the same time.

Hoplosternum thoracatum — Port Hoplo, Atipa

This catfish occurs over much of northern and central South America east of the Andes Mountains. Adults are too large for most smaller home aquariums, yet juveniles (perhaps a group of three to five) make ideal community tank specimens. They are peaceful, robust, and are clearly different from catfishes of the genus *Corydoras*. Even the reproductive biology is substantially different. *Hoplosternum thoracatum* builds a bubblenest and the male cares for the brood. However, breeding can really be accomplished only in a specially set up breeding tank.

The port hoplo is essentially nocturnal, and only after the onset of darkness does it become active. It is an omnivorous species that also requires an area where it can "dig" uninhibitedly. Adequate hiding places must always be provided.

The water level in the tank should be kept low. A heavy plant cover provides the reduced light levels needed by this species to bring out its best qualities. It should be kept in a tank with South American tetras. However, it can also be a suitable companion for rainbowfishes, livebearers, and barbs.

°C

30
29
28
27
26
25
24
23
22
21
20
19

Top: The port hoplo, *Hoplosternum thoracatum,* is peaceful and easy to keep although larger than *Corydoras* species. Unlike corydoras cats, which lay their eggs on the glass or leaves, *Hoplosternum* species build bubblenests much like those of bettas. **Bottom:** *Pseudocrenilabrus multicolor,* the familiar dwarf Egyptian mouthbrooder, is very colorful when mating.

Family Cichlidae

(East Africa: shaded waters)
Pseudocrenilabrus *multicolor* — Dwarf Egyptian Mouthbrooder

This was one of the first cichlid species intensively studied for its reproductive behavior. The female—somewhat less colorful than the male—picks up the eggs and incubates them in her mouth cavity. Only after the young are capable of swimming on their own will the mother release them. However, in the event of danger the young quickly return to the safety of their mother's mouth. This interesting brood behavior can sometimes be observed in a large, thinly populated community tank. The aggressive male should be removed after spawning has been completed. Yet, even without breeding them, these peaceful cichlids are lots of fun to observe. They establish regular territories and are very active without being rough toward each other or other tank inhabitants. Even plants are not uprooted by dwarf Egyptian mouthbrooders.

The maximum size of this species is about 3 inches. It is widely distributed throughout eastern Africa from Egypt south to Tanzania but it is found primarily in tributaries of the River Nile. Nowadays almost all dwarf Egyptian mouthbrooders sold are exclusively hatchery bred; direct imports of this species are rare.

Vallisneria and *Aponogeton* are the most suitable plants for a tank with *P. multicolor*. Hiding places should be provided in the form of halved coconut shells, small flowerpots turned upside down, or rocky caves. Planting must not be

°C
30
29
28
27
26
25
24
23
22
21
20
19

Mouthbrooding cichlids occur in many genera from both Africa and South America, but the little dwarf Egyptian mouthbrooder is still one of the most attractive and easily kept of the mouthbrooders. Since the female cares for the young in her mouth until they are old enough to fend for themselves, successfully raising the fry is easy.

too dense, and there has to be an area along the bottom with fine sand.

This species is essentially omnivorous, although live food is definitely preferred. Coinhabitants for a couple of pairs of dwarf Egyptian mouthbrooders should be selected on the basis of whether they leave the mouthbrooders in peace. It is best to select species that inhabit the upper or middle regions of the tank. Best suited are South American tetras (which also prefer somewhat lower water temperatures), livebearers, or White Clouds. Although this would mean the community tank contains fish from three continents (South America, Asia and Africa), all of them are quite compatible and their requirements are largely the same.

(Africa: along banks of forest streams)
Pelvicachromis pulcher — Kribensis
(formerly Pelmatochromis kribensis)

°C

| 30 |
| 29 |
| 28 |
| 27 |
| 26 |
| 25 |
| 24 |
| 23 |
| 22 |
| 21 |
| 20 |
| 19 |

This undemanding cichlid from tropical western Africa (males about 3 ¾ inches and females about 3 inches) is much more peaceful than most of its relatives. Therefore, it can be used to fill the bottom region of a community tank. It requires reduced light levels with plenty of hiding places; roots, plant thickets, and caves provide a satisfactory environment for this fish. Artificial rocky structures have to be built solidly so that they do not cave in under the busy digging activities of this species. In order to cater to this habit, at least some sections of the bottom should be relatively soft.

It is advisable to keep this fish in pairs only or one male with two females. The middle and upper regions of the tank are then filled with such species as tetras or rainbowfishes.

Top: The kribensis, *Pelvicachromis pulcher,* is a familiar and easy to keep cichlid that is called *Pelmatochromis kribensis* in the old literature. The female develops a brilliant pinkish purple belly when ready to breed. **Bottom:** *Hemichromis thomasi* is an attractive little African cichlid that is unknown to most aquarists.

Males can be recognized by their obviously extended dorsal and anal fins. The "eyespots" in the upper half of the tail are also characteristic of males and can range from one to five in number.

Both parents take part in the brood care; they are cave brooders. Sometimes it is possible to rear at least a few young in a community tank, but the tank has to be large and contain only a few other fishes. Then most of the other fishes will actually avoid the breeding pair, because at that time they can be a bit aggressive.

This species feeds on a variety of live foods, preferring water fleas, tubifex worms, cyclops, and mosquito larvae. Occasionally it also takes some plant food.

Hemichromis thomasi — African Butterfly Cichlid
(Formerly *Pelmatochromis thomasi*)

°C

30
29
28
27
26
25
23
22
21
20
19

This species is widely distributed throughout Sierra Leone. It does well in a community tank when kept under the same conditions as *Pelvicachromis pulcher*, yet it looks very different from the kribensis. The sexes can be distinguished only during the breeding season, at which time females have a distinctly heavier body. By comparison, *Hemichromis thomasi* seems to be even more peaceful than the kribensis. It also has a tendency to spawn more commonly in community tanks. The juveniles are at first silvery in color, lacking the attractive coloration of the adults, in which the glistening turquoise dots covering the entire body are so conspicuous.

Aquarists need not be alarmed if a butterfly cichlid appears to have vanished from the tank! If threatened, *H. thomasi* will quickly bury itself sideways into the sand.

Top: *Hemichromis bimaculatus* is a very commonly seen aquarium species famous for its bright red color, but it is quite aggressive. **Middle:** Long considered to be a pale phase of *Hemichromis bimaculatus,* this fish is now considered by many scientists to perhaps be a distinct species. **Bottom:** *Hemichromis thomasi* is a very peaceful species compared to *H. bimaculatus* and is not unattractive, but it has few really distinctive characters.

(South America: along riverbanks)
Apistogramma borelli — High-finned Dwarf Cichlid
(formerly *A. reitzigi*)

With a maximum size of 2 inches for females and over 3 inches for males, this species is indeed a dwarf among cichlids, so it can be kept in any community tank without hesitation. The bottom of the tank should be left exclusively to this fish so that it can establish its territories and pursue in uninhibited fashion its normal cichlid behavior pattern. If the overall conditions are favorable it may even breed occasionally in a community tank.

Apistogramma borelli broods its eggs in caves. Brood care is done primarily by the female, while the male defends the territory. However, to protect the tiny brood against the hungry mouths of barbs or tetras is simply too much of a task for even the most dedicated *borelli* females.

The tank habitat for this species must be as variable as its natural habitat in South America — hiding places are needed in the form overturned flowerpots, halved coconut shells, roots, and rocks. Water plants are permitted since high-finned dwarf cichlids generally go easy on plants. Some open swimming space is also required. The bottom must be soft and preferably dark in color.

This is a largely omnivorous species, but live food is definitely preferred. When feeding a community tank that contains some *A. borelli*, special attention must be paid that sufficient food falls to the bottom for them.

The sexes can easily be distinguished by coloration and size differences. The large males are clearly more attractive, with bright colors. Their pectoral fins are more pointed,

°C

| 30 |
| 29 |
| 28 |
| 27 |
| 26 |
| 25 |
| 24 |
| 23 |
| 22 |
| 21 |
| 20 |
| 19 |

Top: Recently many new species of *Apistogramma* have been described, and the names of others have been changed. *A. reitzigi* of older literature is now called *A. borelli*, but regardless of the name used, the high dorsal fin and simple color pattern are distinctive. **Bottom:** When spawning, the male golden dwarf cichlid, *Nannacara anomala,* develops a beautiful iridescent pattern.

and the posterior rays of the dorsal and anal fins are prominently extended (as opposed to being rounded off in females). A female ready to spawn turns bright yellow. When both partners are excited dark bars appear across their bodies.

It is advisable to keep only one pair in a medium sized tank since territorial fighting may occur if more than one male is present. The upper regions of the tank should preferably be filled with neon tetras. Close to the surface can be put *Rasbora dorsiocellata* or *Thayeria boehlkei*.

Nannacara anomala — Golden Dwarf Cichlid, Checkerboard Dwarf Cichlid

This peaceful and active cichlid from some of the smaller, heavily vegetated streams of northern South America can be kept in any community tank without having any detrimental effect on the other tank inhabitants. However, it is important to not add any other bottom-dwellers to a tank with a pair of *Nannacara anomala*. Moreover, one of the partners should be exchanged if fighting occurs among them. It should be noted here that unlike many other cichlids, *N. anomala* does not maintain permanent pair bonds. Other fishes for inclusion in such a community are the same as listed for *Apistogramma borelli*.

The checkerboard dwarf cichlid forms territories and indicates its "mood" by its coloration. This is particularly noticeable in a female when she is taking care of her brood (checkerboard pattern) or if she is angry (bright colors). Fully grown males (about 3½ inches long) are very much more colorful than adult females (about 2½ inches). The

°C
30
29
28
27
26
25
23
22
21
20
19

Male golden dwarf cichlids are territorial when ready to spawn and will fight with other males, as well as chase off any other fishes that enter their domain. They are best kept only a pair to a tank, and many aquarists suggest removing the male after spawning is finished.

bottom of the tank must be carefully prepared for this species: use elodea for the planting and provide caves, halved coconut shells, or overturned flowerpots for cover.

Family Cobitidae

(Southeast Asia: streams and ditches)
Acanthophthalmus kuhlii — **Kuhli Loach**

The kuhli loach requires relatively high temperatures and prefers a dimly lighted environment. In appearance it is more worm-like than fish-like. This species lives almost exclusively on the bottom and even *IN* the bottom. Therefore, a soft substrate (sand or some peat moss) should be available for it to dig into for food and cover. *A. kuhlii* is primarily nocturnal, so it becomes active only after the onset of darkness. Adequate hiding places such as caves, thick plants, or roots are mandatory.

This species must have contact to others of its own kind, so it should never be kept by itself but instead kept in small groups. *A. kuhlii* tends to be somewhat shy, at least until it has become firmly adjusted to a community tank, so it is not advisable to add to the same tank other bottom-dwellers that could upset the loach. Quiet fishes of the middle or upper zone are more suitable as companions. Although loaches can find a lot of edible material in the sand and gravel, it is imperative that sufficient food reaches the bottom and does not get eaten by the other fishes on the way down. It may be prudent for the hobbyist to feed all the other fishes first and then give additional food to the kuhli

°C
30
29
28
27
26
25
24
23
22
21
20
19

Top: The most commonly seen kuhli loach is *Acanthophthalmus kuhli,* but other similar species are often imported, including the *A. myersi* pictured. Actually, the kuhli loaches are all very similar in pattern and there is much variation, making species hard to distinguish. **Bottom:** The half-banded loach, *Acanthophthalmus semicinctus,* can be kept like any other kuhli.

32

loaches on the bottom. Small worms are the preferred food, and dried food is also eagerly taken once the fish have become adapted to it.

This species reaches a maximum length about 5 inches and has considerable longevity in the aquarium. If a fish seems to have disappeared for a few days there is nothing to worry about — suddenly it reappears from its hiding place and races along with the other loaches. It is important that the tank is *TIGHTLY* covered, because *A. kuhlii* has a tendency to "slide up" the glass (particularly in corners) and end up on the floor.

The sexes are difficult or impossible to distinguish though there are small differences in the shape and structure of the fins. During the breeding season the female becomes distinctly heavier. This fish rarely breeds in aquaria.

A. kuhlii occurs throughout Thailand to Indonesia (one of the main collecting areas is the island of Sumatra) and lives in slowly flowing streams and ditches with soft, muddy bottoms. Plant cover is sparse and most likely to be floating plants such as duckweed (*Lemna*) and azolla.

Compatible occupants for such a community tank are other Southeast Asian fishes such as *Rasbora heteromorpha* and gouramis.

The pattern of this species varies considerably, and several subspecies or color varieties have been described, but the validity of these other names is uncertain.

In the event a loach is threatened with imminent danger, a tiny spine just below the eye serves as an effective defense weapon. A similar spine, often with a swivelling base, is found in many other loaches.

Since kuhli loaches are bottom-fishes and are usually on or in the substrate, compatible fishes for their aquarium would be species that inhabit the middle and upper waters of the tank, such as the harlequin rasbora, *Rasbora heteromorpha,* shown here. European aquarists believe that all the fishes in an aquarium should come from the same area, so they would never place an American tetra with an Asian loach.

°C

Acanthophthalmus semicinctus —
Half-banded Loach

This is a close relative of *A. kuhlii* that can be kept under identical conditions. It has slightly different markings, and the maximum size is only a bit over 3 inches.

There are still other similar species of kuhli loaches distinguished somewhat doubtfully by color pattern. The pet trade invariably sells all species as just "kuhli loaches," so a close search may reveal several different species in the same tank.

Botia macracantha — Clown Loach

The clown loach is imported primarily from Sumatra and Borneo (both highlands and flooded lowland areas), where it reaches a maximum length of a foot. In a large community tank it may reach a size of about 5 inches. It is quite compatible with many smaller species, such as similarly colored tiger barbs or harlequin rasboras. Aquarists have at times observed that clown loaches kept individually can be aggressive, yet they will behave quite differently when in a small group of four to six fish.

Clown loaches prefer a tank with a large bottom area and with subdued lighting and at least some soft substrate for digging into and burying themselves (sand or peat moss is good). The water level should not be too high. Caves and other hiding places (roots, halved coconut shells) must also be provided for the well-being of clown loaches. With proper care this species can reach a considerable age in captivity. Feeding does not present any problems as clown loaches will eat virtually anything, though some vegetable matter

Top: *Botia macracantha*, the clown loach, is a highly desirable addition to the aquarium because of its exquisite coloring. **Bottom:** The checkerboard loach, *Botia sidthimunki*, seldom greatly exceeds 2 inches in length, so it can be kept with quite small species.

must be provided. The food has to be nutritious, and live food should be given periodically. Worms are a favorite food. As with other bottom fishes, care has to be taken that sufficient food actually reaches the bottom where the loaches can then easily detect it with their barbels. Males and females have no distinguishing external characteristics.

Botia sidthimunki — Checkerboard Loach

With a maximum size of only 2½ inches, this is the smallest relative of the clown loach. It has essentially the same requirements and thus can live in the bottom of nearly any community tank. The principal collecting region for this species is in Thailand, where it occurs in slowly flowing streams.

B. sidthimunki is slightly more active than B. macracantha, and it has a tendency to pace up and down the glass. Moreover, it digs untiringly into the bottom substrate, which can cause slight temporary water cloudiness. Thus it is unwise to add other species with similar behavior to the same tank. This species must be kept in a small school; individually kept specimens are rarely ever that active.

The food of course has to fit the small size of the fish's mouth. The checkerboard loach prefers live food such as tubifex worms.

This species has allegedly been bred in captivity, but details are unknown. It is possible that it may not reach sexual maturity under aquarium conditions. It is also said that sometimes unscrupulous exporters ship only one sex of a particular species (including this one) in order to prevent large-scale hatchery breeding.

°C
30
29
28
27
26
25
24
23
22
21
20
19

Loaches tend to feed on the bottom, and these Botia macracantha are no exceptions to the rule. However, a small school of clown loaches will often leave the bottom to swim just below midwater. and they can be very active. The erectile spine under the eye helps protect them from being eaten by larger fishes.

Special care has to be taken when a loach is caught in a net; the tiny spine underneath the eye can inflict painful bleeding puncture wounds. The Thai people call *Botia* "boar fish" because the spines are to them reminiscent of a wild boar's tusks.

Family Cyprinidae

Southeast Asia: mountain streams
***Labeo bicolor* — Red-tailed black Shark**

This is a rather hardy long-lived fish that prefers water plant thickets, roots, caves, and other convenient hiding places. This preference has to be catered to in an aquarium if the fish is to be happy and contented. It is also more active under subdued lighting. Once a territory has been established it is vigorously defended, particularly against other sharks. Consequently, only single specimens should be kept, particularly if the tank is small. Some aquarium literature suggests that several juveniles be permitted to grow up together in the same tank to establish a fairly peaceful group of fish. Obviously, every aquarist has to develop his own experience on this. In any event, the larger the tank and the more hiding places there are for this fish, the more harmony there will be in the long run.

The red-tailed black shark gets along well with other species and is actually a good candidate for most community tanks, where it is quite compatible with barbs, livebearers, and tetras.

°C
30
29
28
27
26
25
24
23
22
21
20
19

Top: The contrasting black and red pattern of the red-tailed black shark, *Labeo bicolor,* helps make it one of the most recognizable of tropical fishes. **Bottom:** Almost every pet shop stocks Chinese algae-eaters, although the specimens are usually small. *Gyrinocheilus aymonieri* makes a worthy addition to any community tank.

40

Labeo bicolor occurs in Thailand, where it lives primarily in streams and rivers, but it is also found occasionally in standing waters. Maximum size in the wild seems to be about 12 inches, yet this fish does not get larger than about 5 inches in most aquaria. It is a typical omnivore feeding on a wide range of items, but the diet must include some vegetable matter such as thoroughly washed boiled spinach leaves or plant-based dried foods. *Labeo bicolor* is also an excellent "algae-eater." A good indicator of the fish's well-being is its velvety black coloration. Little is known about its breeding and reproductive behavior, though it has occasionally been bred in aquaria.

Family Gyrinocheilidae

Gyrinocheilus aymonieri — Chinese Algae-eater

As the common name indicates, this fish feeds largely on algae. In its native Thailand (not China!) it occurs in fast-flowing mountain streams and rivers, where it attaches itself with its sucking mouth onto rocks to prevent being swept away by currents. *Gyrinocheilus* requires a well-aerated tank with plenty of hiding places in the form of roots and plant thickets.

This species can tolerate extremes of temperatures, so it can be used in different types of aquaria, with one or two in a tank to help control algae. It is generally peaceful, although sometimes older specimens tend to "bother" some of the other fishes; that is, the fish not only clean the glass of algae but may also attach themselves to other larger fishes.

Gyrinocheilus is alleged to grow to about 10 inches in the wild, yet aquarium specimens rarely ever exceed 5 inches, and even that takes quite some time to reach. If there is plenty of algae about in the tank no supplementary food is required, although some occasional dried food is appreciated. However, even a single algae-eater will rapidly eat all the algae in a small tank and will then starve if not fed.

°C

30
29
28
27
26
25
24
23
22
21
20
19

Top: Red-tailed black sharks are seldom bred in captivity, although some specialists are now using hormones to assist in spawning the species in captivity. Adults are fairly large and territorial. **Bottom:** One of the major problems with keeping algae-eaters is that they rapidly eat all the natural algae and then have to be fed just like any other fish. It is always wise to feed algae-eaters, catfishes, and other scavengers just like normal fishes.

SCHOOLING FISHES ABOVE THE BOTTOM

Family Melanotaeniidae

°C

Melanotaenia maccullochi — Australian Dwarf Rainbowfish, McCulloch's Rainbowfish

30
29
28
27
26
25
24
23
22
21
20
19

Most of the more popular aquarium fishes are native to Southeast Asia and South America; new species that are suitable for aquaria also continue to be discovered in Africa, yet only a very few aquarium fishes have ever come from Australia. One of these is the brightly colored Dwarf Rainbowfish, an ideal aquarium fish. The maximum size is just over 3 inches.

This is a very active fish that prefers to stay close to the bottom. It can be kept together with other species that also require only moderate temperatures and prefer a tank with lots of swimming space not cluttered up by lots of plants.

Top: Traditionally several species of Australian rainbowfishes have been imported for the aquarium market, but only *Melanotaenia macullochi* could be considered well established in the hobby. **Bottom:** The glowlight tetra, *Hemigrammus erythrozonus*, is one of the most attractive of the small tetras.

Tetras, barbs, and livebearers are the most suitable companions for rainbowfishes. The bottom of such a community tank can contain catfishes and loaches.

Dwarf rainbowfish are omnivorous feeders. They can be bred easily, but not very successfully, in a community tank. The female is somewhat paler in coloration than the male, which has characteristically extended, pointed posterior dorsal and anal fins. Juveniles are less colorful than their parents; only mature fish show the typical "rainbow" colors.

Several other rainbowfishes from Australia and New Guinea are now on the market. Many are colorful and quite suited to the community aquarium.

Family Characidae

°C

| 30 |
| 29 |
| 28 |
| 27 |
| 26 |
| 25 |
| 24 |
| 23 |
| 22 |
| 21 |
| 20 |
| 19 |

(South America: forest streams and rivers)
Hemigrammus erythrozonus **— Glowlight Tetra**
(Formerly — incorrectly — *Hyphessobrycon gracilis*)

Glowlight tetras are found from the forest rivers of Guyana to the savannah streams of Paraguay. As a "glowing" tetra it goes very well together with a tank full of neon tetras to produce a rain forest theme. Hyperactive fishes should not be included in this sort of community tank because they would disturb these small (1⅔ inches long), quiet fish. A tropical rain forest aquarium should have a dark bottom, possibly with a thin peat moss layer, and the surface of the water should be covered with floating plants so that very little light can penetrate to the bottom. There-

Top: Formerly—and very appropriately—called *Hemigrammus gracilis* or *Hyphessobrycon gracilis*, a school of glowlight tetras on a dark gravel substrate with dim lighting seems to literally glow in the dark. **Bottom:** Recently the spectacular New Guinea red rainbowfish, *Glossolepis incisus*, has come onto the aquarium market and attracted a large following.

fore, any water plants used must be selected specifically to tolerate reduced light levels. Glowlight tetras are not very active swimmers; more typically they remain quietly among the plants.

The sexes are hard to distinguish by coloration alone, but older females have more rounded abdomens. It takes some experience to distinguish males and females by body shape alone. As far as food is concerned glowlight tetras are undemanding omnivorous feeders with some preference for live foods. They require very clean water, and they seem to be somewhat more susceptible to diseases than most other tetras.

(South America: shaded banks of forest streams)
Paracheirodon innesi — Neon Tetra

This amazing fish was discovered in 1936 in the upper reaches of the Amazon (Rio Ucayali in Peru) and immediately became a very popular aquarium tetra.

Neon tetras are ideally suited for a community tank, yet they should never be kept together with larger fishes (even angelfish may occasionally swallow a small neon tetra). Experienced aquarists also consider it to be imprudent to keep neon tetras together with rasboras since the tetra prefers somewhat cooler water than rasboras. However, water temperature of about 75 °F should be a suitable compromise for both the South American and Southeast Asian species.

The 1 4/5-inch neon tetra is esthetically most pleasing when kept as a large school of 10 to 20 fish. The bottom of the community tank can be filled with corydoras catfishes. Also very attractive is a group of penguins *(Thayeria)* near the surface. Livebearers are really not suited for such a community tank.

°C
30
29
28
27
26
25
24
23
22
21
20
19

Neon tetras **(top)** and cardinal tetras **(bottom)** are often confused by beginners. The cardinal tetra, *Paracheirodon axelrodi*, has the broad red stripe continued far forward on the body, often reaching the gill covers. In the neon, *P. innesi*, the red stripe stops under the dorsal fin.

48

Neon tetras require a fair amount of swimming space, but the sides and back of the tank should be planted densely, perhaps with *Echinodorus, Aponogeton, Cryptocorynes,* and *Cabomba.* Floating plants will reduce the light level somewhat; the bottom should be dark (use basalt gravel, possibly also some peat moss) and the back wall should also be of a dark color. Some well-soaked driftwood is also very decorative. As far as food is concerned, neons are not particularly choosy, but the diet should be varied and must include small live foods.

Females can often be recognized by fuller abdomens if they are mature, and males have slightly indented "throats" (not a very reliable characteristic).

The single disadvantage of keeping this fish is its susceptibility to the so-called neon tetra disease, in which the red band becomes discolored and grayish. Affected specimens should immediately be removed and destroyed.

°C

30
29
28
27
26
25
24
23
22
21
20
19

Paracheirodon axelrodi — Cardinal Tetra

The cardinal tetra — imported as an aquarium fish for the first time as late as 1956 — is a typical small tetra of "black water" Amazon streams. It was first found in the Rio Negro region. The typical amber color of rivers in this region is derived from decaying leaves, branches, and roots of plants that accumulate in dry river beds during the dry season; these river beds become deeply flooded during the wet season. Aquarium fish shops have commercially prepared substances for sale that darken the aquarium water and change the water quality slightly in order to simulate conditions in a typical tropical black water forest stream. Yet the most

A school of cardinal tetras has to rank as one of the most beautiful sights in the fish world. Although a single fish is not conspicuous, a dozen or more in a dark tank make the aquarium come alive with color.

important thing to remember is that the water must be clean and perfectly clear. Some aquarists insist on using humic and/or tannic acid additives to lower the pH and possibly soften the water, but others believe the fish will show their best coloration only in normal tap water.

Family Cyprinidae

Puntius conchonius — Rosy Barb

The rosy barb occurs in streams, ponds, and water holes in northern and eastern India as well as in Bangladesh. It is a type of fish that likes to dig around the bottom, a fact that must be taken into consideration when the tank is set up; at least some of the bottom area must consist of soft sand. The maximum size of this species is about 3 inches. It is an active fish that requires lots of swimming space, but the sides and back of the tank should be densely planted with *Vallisneria, Cryptocoryne,* or *Limnophila.* About a quarter of the aquarium's water surface should be covered with some floating plants such as *Azolla* or *Lemna* since the fish sometimes prefer areas with subdued lighting.

Rosy barbs are hardy fish that can even be kept outdoors during the warm summer months. Their coloration intensifies with higher water temperatures. They are truly omnivorous in feeding requirements (as indeed are most barbs), but they must have some vegetable matter in their diet. During the breeding season the male turns bright

°C
30
29
28
27
26
25
24
23
22
21
20
19

Top: Rosy barbs, *Puntius conchonius,* are very hardy fish that can even survive warm summers in outdoor ponds. Females are relatively plain compared to the males shown. **Bottom:** A spawning black ruby barb, *Puntius nigrofasciatus,* is a striking fish.

pinkish red and the dorsal fin gets a black margin. The female can be recognized by her fuller abdomen and bright silvery coloration. This barb will readily breed in captivity.

The rosy barb has been a popular aquarium fish since way back in 1903. It is very compatible with other barbs of the same general size as well as with the various gourami species. When kept at lower temperatures, White Clouds also go well with rosy barbs. However, the lively, rather active barbs should not be put together with some of the more quiet and sedate fishes if these occupy the same level and region in a community tank. Rosy barbs must not be kept at temperatures above 77 °F. When properly cared for they can live about three years in an aquarium.

(Southeast Asia: forest and mountain streams)
Puntius nigrofasciatus — **Black Ruby Barb**

°C

	30
	29
	28
	27
	26
	25
	24
	23
	22
	21
	20
	19

"Durable," "robust," and "rather undemanding" best describe the 2-inch black ruby barb from Sri Lanka. This species generally inhabits densely overgrown shallow water regions of slowly flowing or even standing waters. Apart from the fact that this fish requires higher water temperatures than rosy barbs, the same care and maintenance requirements apply. Black ruby barbs are also ideally suited for a community tank, not only in conjunction with other Asian fishes but also with fishes from South America and Africa, provided the maintenance requirements are the same. It is advisable to place the tank in a position that is not too bright; this brings out the colors of these barbs far more effectively.

Female black ruby barbs **(top)** are far from unattractive fishes, but the spawning male **(bottom)** with its bright red and black coloration and black fins is unique. A long-finned variety has recently been developed.

During the breeding season the male gets a pattern of dark vertical bands against a nearly purplish red background. When such a fish becomes excited (*e.g.*, during intra-specific "sparring" between two males), the colors intensify even further. When not in breeding color this species has a light-colored body, while the head in mature males and females becomes bright red. The body colors of females are generally more subdued; their fins are transparent with only a tinge of color.

Generally, black ruby barbs tend to live quite a long time, with proper care reaching at least 8 years. They require a nutritious, varied diet (live and frozen foods should be included) in order to show their best colors and to reach breeding condition.

(Southeast Asia: rivers, streams, and lakes)
Capoeta oligolepis — **Checker Barb**

°C

30
29
28
27
26
25
24
23
22
21
20
19

This active 2-inch-long barb lives in rapidly flowing shallow streams and rivers of Sumatra. It may not be quite as colorful as rosy or ruby barbs, but it does provide a conspicuous contrast when all three are kept in the same tank. The checker barb shows off most effectively under subdued lighting, as under a cover of floating plants. Loaches can occupy the bottom in such a tank, while a couple of pairs of *Trichogaster* live in the upper water zone.

Checker barbs will feed on nearly anything, yet the best growth and condition is obtained with a nutritious, varied diet that must include vegetable matter as well as live foods. Males sometimes tend to fight, though without inflicting

Top: The simple but attractive pattern of the checkered barb, *Capoeta oligolepis*, has its admirers, but its main advantage is that it is very easy to keep. **Bottom:** The half-striped barb, *Capoeta "schuberti,"* is rather a mystery, as no one seems to agree on whether it is a good species or an aquarium variety of *C. sachsi* or *C. semifasciolatus.*

any serious damage upon each other. The copper-colored dorsal and anal fins with the typical black margin are characteristic of males. In females these fins are yellowish.

C. oligolepis was introduced into the aquarium fish trade in 1914. Breeding is fairly easy, but a well matched compatible pair is essential for breeding success. Care and maintenance are the same as for the rosy and black ruby barbs.

Capoeta (semifasciolatus) "schuberti"—Half-striped Barb

°C

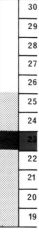

Possibly a mutation of the rarely seen Hong Kong barb (also known as the green barb, semi barb, and half-banded barb), the origin of this attractive barb is a mystery. It is definitely not found in the wild, however. Many ichthyologists are of the opinion that it could be a yellow (xanthistic) mutant of *Capoeta semifasciolatus*, which occurs in southeastern China. Others consider it to be a mutation of the goldfin barb, *Capoeta sachsi*.

This fish was observed for the first time in progeny raised by Tom Schubert in the 1950's. He developed it into a pure-bred variety and then exported some of these fish to Europe. It is a fairly robust fish but is not known as being very active. Females have a somewhat plumper shape than males, and instead of the dark longitudinal band there are usually only some dark spots. The maximum size is almost 3 inches.

Tank decoration, care, and maintenance are the same as described for other barb species. This fish does not breed very willingly.

Top: *Capoeta semifasciolatus* and *C sachsi* are perhaps the same species. Many aquarists feel that this is the parent species of *C. "schuberti."* **Bottom:** Tiger barbs are among the most popular of barbs. Recently several aquarium varieties have been developed that are striking in their beauty, including this albino tiger barb.

(Southeast Asia: standing and running waters)
Capoeta tetrazona — Tiger Barb, Sumatra Barb

High on the scale of favorites among aquarium hobbyists is the tiger barb, which can be found on most of the Indonesian islands. They can be kept in a community tank, provided one refrains from keeping long-finned fishes with them, because the tiger barb is unjustifiably suspected of pulling to pieces and nibbling on the flowing fins of angelfish and gouramis. If only one or two tiger barbs are kept, they do become unfriendly with other species in the tank, which is why keeping at least a half dozen is recommended. Tiger barbs can adapt to many different conditions, but one should remember that the colors are most beautiful at temperatures of about 75°F or even warmer. All too often one sees tiger barbs in the company of fishes kept cooler, the hobbyist having no idea that they would develop much better at somewhat higher temperatures.

°C

30
29
28
27
26
25
24
23
22
21
20
19

In the aquarium tiger barbs will reach at most 3 inches in length. They need plenty of swimming space, but plants can be used, especially different *Cryptocoryne* species or clumps of moss or fern. A cover of floating plants is likewise recommended.

Tiger barbs are really greedy. They will eat almost anything but must be given live foods to breed. The males can be distinguished from the females by being much redder and more slender; during breeding season the upper part of the body is bright red. Very similar in appearance to the partly banded barb.

Top: *Capoeta tetrazona,* the tiger barb, is found in every aquarium shop and is one of the most popular fish species. However, they are often fin-nippers and can drive a slow-moving long-finned fish, such as an anglefish, crazy. **Bottom:** Spawning cherry barbs, *Capoeta titteya,* are pinkish in spawning females and brilliant red in spawning males.

Capoeta titteya — Cherry Barb

°C

| 30 |
| 29 |
| 28 |
| 27 |
| 26 |
| 25 |
| **24** |
| 23 |
| 22 |
| 21 |
| 20 |
| 19 |

The 2-inch-long cherry barb occurs in shady streams and small rivers in Sri Lanka. Aquarium specimens are sometimes a bit shy and have a tendency to hide among plants. It prefers subdued lighting and the company of fishes that are not too active. The diet must include some vegetable matter; soft algae are often eagerly eaten.

During the breeding season the male (more slender than the female) becomes an intense red, while the female remains pale pinkish. Cherry barbs should be kept under the same conditions as listed for other members of this genus. It is ideally suited for a community tank. Very compatible with this barb are gouramis (which could be molested by tiger barbs).

MID-WATER SCHOOLING FISHES

Family Characidae

°C

| 30 |
| 29 |
| 28 |
| 27 |
| 26 |
| 25 |
| 24 |
| 23 |
| **22** |
| 21 |
| 20 |
| 19 |

(South America: rivers and streams)
Aphyocharax anisitsi-Bloodfin, Red-finned Tetra
(formerly *A. rubripinnis*)

This peaceful, active fish can tolerate—at least temporarily—relatively low temperatures since it occurs fairly far south (Argentina) in South America. It is widely distributed throughout the Rio Parana and Rio de la Plata regions. The maximum size is 2 inches.

Males and females are identical in coloration, but the male has a slighter more slender body. Breeding is not difficult.

62

Top: The bloodfin, *Aphyocharax anisitsi*. **Bottom:** The silver tetra, *Ctenobrycon spilurus*.

As an active swimmer, the bloodfin requires a good bit of open space. The tank must not be too densely planted; in fact, there need to be only a few plants such as *Cabomba, Heteranthera,* or *Elodea* along the sides and back. The fish often spends some time near the surface. It requires quite a bit of patience and skill to catch these fish to remove them from an aquarium. One has to proceed with caution so that the fish does not become entangled in the net. Preferably any netting operation should be done in the late evening when the aquarium is already dark.

If the tank is sufficiently large another species can be added, possibly also in the form of a small school that would occupy the lower water region. A rainbowfish would be very suitable for that purpose. Although rainbowfishes come from Australia, they have about the same care and maintenance requirements as the bloodfin and are just as peaceful and compatible.

Ctenobrycon spilurus — Silver Tetra

°C

30
29
28
27
26
25
24
23
22
21
20
19

The silver tetra occurs in coastal rivers of northern South America (Venezuela and Guyana), where it lives in shallow inshore bays. It is a rather active fish that attains a maximum length of about 3 3/5 inches. Although generally peaceful, it should not be kept together with much smaller fishes because some specimens can become somewhat aggressive toward smaller fishes.

The silver tetra should be given a large, long tank where the sides and back are well-planted with *Heteranthera, Ludwigia,* or *Cabomba.* The food supply has to be abundant and regular, with dried and live foods included.

The female is generally somewhat heavier than the male and sometimes also a bit longer. In comparison with many

Aquarists commonly recognize two subspecies of silver tetras, *Ctenobrycon spilurus hauxwellianus* **(top)** and *C. s. spilurus* **(bottom)**, but the value of using these names for almost identical fish is doubtful.

64

...From T.F.H., the world's largest publisher of bird books, a new bird magazine for birdkeepers all over the world...

CAGED BIRD HOBBYIST
IS FOR EVERYONE
WHO LOVES BIRDS.

CAGED BIRD HOBBYIST
IS PACKED WITH VALUABLE
INFORMATION SHOWING HOW
TO FEED, HOUSE, TRAIN AND CARE
FOR ALL TYPES OF BIRDS.

Subscribe right now so you don't miss a single copy!   SM-316

other tetras the silver tetra is indeed plain, but it makes up for this with its spectacular courtship behavior. Ideally, a school of silver tetras should be raised together from juveniles. Breeding *C. spilurus* in a community tank is not likely to succeed. The young require an incubation and hatching temperature of about 79°F, which is not recommended for the normal maintenance of this species.

(South America: rivers)
Gymnocorymbus ternetzi — Black Tetra

This species occurs in the swamp lands of the upper reaches of the Rio Paraguay. It requires some open swimming space, but at times it also likes to be among thick plants such as *Vallisneria, Heteranthera, Sagittaria,* or *Myriophyllum.*

The black tetra often establishes loose territories that are sometimes even defended against intruders. Older fish, as remainders from an earlier school in the same tank, should be removed because they may become aggressive. Juveniles are velvety black, but older specimens become more of a dark grayish and are less attractive. By applying special methods, experienced aquarists can often prolong the attractive appearance even in older black tetras. The somewhat smaller male has a white-tipped tail, while the female's remains colorless; such small differences are often hard to detect.

This species is essentially omnivorous, feeding on all sorts of foods. The diet should be varied, including both dried and live foods. Prolonged feeding with dried food will do no harm to black tetras. Mosquito larvae are a favorite food.

°C
30
29
28
27
26
25
24
23
22
21
20
19

The black tetra, *Gymnocorymbus ternetzi,* is one of many aquarium fishes that have developed long-finned varieties under aquarium conditions. The long-finned black tetra, sometimes called the GTO, is one of the more popular long-finned fishes.

66

Most compatible with black tetras in a community tank are *Hyphessobrycon flammeus* and other *Hyphessobrycon* and *Hemigrammus* species, as well as *Pristella maxillaris*. The bottom of such a tank can be stocked with corydoras catfishes. It is generally advisable to have a larger school of a single tetra species rather than a few individuals of several different tetra species. This affords better opportunities for observing the typical behavior patterns of a particular species.

Hemigrammus caudovittatus — Buenos Aires Tetra

This very undemanding species from around Buenos Aires, Argentina, is an ideal aquarium fish. However, care has to be taken that it does not chew on aquarium plants — vegetable matter such as frozen spinach, tender lettuce leaves, and chlorophyll-containing dried foods must be included in its diet. For this reason it may not be advisable to include fine-leaved or feathery plants in a tank destined to accommodate this species. Instead, plants with hard leaves like *Cryptocoryne* may prove to be more durable.

Although *H. caudovittatus* can tolerate lower temperatures for some time, it does display far brighter colors when kept warmer. In a cold-water tank, for instance, there is no indication of the attractiveness of this fish. As in most other tetras, males remain somewhat smaller and more slender than females but show brighter colors.

This is a schooling fish that can reach a maximum size just under 3 inches. Occasionally it can become slightly rough toward smaller fishes, so very small specimens should not be included in a community aquarium with *H. caudovittatus*. There are no problems with larger fishes.

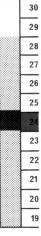

°C

30
29
28
27
26
25
24
23
22
21
20
19

Top: The black tetra, *Gymnocorymbus ternetzi,* is one of the fishes that is best kept in schools. **Bottom:** *Hemigrammus caudovittatus,* the Buenos Aires tetra, will thrive in water that is much cooler than most other aquarium fishes will even tolerate, although it develops little color in cool water.

68

Some aquarists have reported seeing the Buenos Aires tetra chew on the thread-like extended pelvic fins of angelfish and gouramis, but because of different temperature requirements the tetra should not be in the same tank as these other fishes. Unfortunately, this is a point that is not often enough taken into consideration when community tanks are set up.

Hasemania nana — Silver-tipped Tetra

This little fish (maximum size 2 inches, the males slightly smaller) is esthetically only effective when in a large school. The activity pattern varies between turbulent "play-like" chasing to remaining subdued among thickets of *Vallisneria, Ludwigia,* or *Elodea.* Its geographic range includes much of southeastern Brazil, primarily around Rio de Janeiro. The adipose fin found in most other tetras is absent in this species. Like most tetras, *H. nana* is omnivorous, but the diet must occasionally include algae and other tender vegetable matter.

The best companions for this species are those fishes that do not require elevated temperatures. There are many other tetras that fall into this category, so select those that offer distinct color contrasts, not those where shades of red dominate. Some barbs are also quite suitable, and livebearers are also compatible.

°C

30
29
28
27
26
25
24
23
22
21
20
19

(South America: shaded forest rivers and streams)
Hemigrammus ocellifer — Head and Tail Light Tetra

This fish is most advantageously displayed in a community tank patterned after the South American rain forest.

Top: Although it has no bright colors, the bronzy and white silver-tipped tetra, *Hasemania nana,* looks fine in a school. **Bottom:** The head and tail light tetra, *Hemigrammus ocellifer,* looks best as a school in a dark tank.

Indeed, it occurs in dark, shaded forest streams, primarily in Venezuela (the Orinoco region), Guyana, northern Brazil, and the Amazon and its tributaries. It does not prefer the lower regions of the tank (as do neon and glowlight tetras) but instead swims around in the open water, sometimes close to the floating plant cover near the surface.

The maximum size of this schooling fish is 2 inches. It was first introduced to the aquarium hobby in 1910 and has been very popular ever since. There are two forms: *Hemigrammus ocellifer ocellifer*, with a conspicuous shoulder spot; and *H. ocellifer falsus*, which does not possess a shoulder spot.

Males are generally somewhat smaller and more slender than females. The light spot at the base of the tail must serve as a recognition signal in dark forest streams so that the members of a school do not lose contact with each other. *H. ocellifer* will feed on a wide range of items, with cyclops, water fleas, and other small live foods clearly preferred. When caught in a net some of the fish will become entangled. Invariably these are males, which have a tiny hook on the anal fin rays that easily gets caught in the net's webbing.

Hyphessobrycon callistus — Callistus Tetra, Blood Tetra

Fortunately the average aquarist does not have to worry about the complicated systematics of the callistus group of tetras. Their care and requirement are all identical no matter what species is involved. There are a number of mostly poorly defined species and subspecies in this group, and

Deep-bodied red tetras with long-based anal fins are usually just lumped together as serpae tetras, but there are actually quite a few species that fit this description. The fish above is usually called *Hyphessobrycon serpae*, although its true name is arguable. That below is *H. callistus*, the callistus tetra.

72

most tropical fish dealers do not have the correct name(s) for the fish they sell. This state of affairs is not really surprising, since ichthyologists cannot agree among themselves either. The differences are primarily in the overall coloration and the shoulder spot, which may vary from well-defined or totally absent.

The blood tetras are widely distributed throughout South America, from middle Amazonas to the Rio Madeira and Rio Guapore to the spring region in the Mato Grosso area, as well as in the upper reaches of the Rio Paraguay.

Whatever form is selected for a community tank, it will be conspicuous through its superb beauty. The maximum size is about 2½ inches, with males remaining generally smaller than females. By and large they are peaceful fish. However, a few aquarists have reported that sometimes older specimens can become "difficult" and start damaging the fins of other fishes. Such individuals should be removed promptly.

Blood tetras will fit into any community tank that contains fishes with similar temperature requirements. They provide a particularly pleasant contrast against other tetras. These fish need some swimming space but at times also prefer to remain quietly among the plants. The diet must be varied.

(South America: savannah streams and rivers)
Hyphessobrycon flammeus — Flame Tetra, Red Tetra

This species was first discovered in the area around Rio de Janeiro and was introduced into the aquarium hobby in 1920. It has been a favorite among aquarists ever since then. The maximum size is about 1⅔ inches. It is peaceful, very attractive, and undemanding in its care and attention.

Top: *Hyphessobrycon callistus,* the callistus tetra, is recognized by the paleness of the red, the large spot behind the head, and the black and white edges of the anal fin. **Bottom:** Flame tetras, *Hyphessobrycon flammeus,* are one of many tetras available on a sporadic basis. Their colors are just not bright enough to put them in constant demand.

H. *flammeus* is—like most other tetras—a typical omnivore with a preference for live foods. The slightly larger females can be distinguished by the absence of black margins on the anal fin and tips of the pelvic fins. Older aquarists often insist that those *H. flammeus* available now are far less colorful than those in years gone by.

As typical of tetras, *H. flammeus* is most comfortable when among its own kind, though a few older individuals can sometimes get a bit aggressive. During the breeding season the male flame tetra is quite temperamental, so aggressively pursued females must find hiding places. Thus the side and back of the aquarium must be densely planted, leaving some open swimming space in the center. *Brachydanio* species from Southeast Asia are the most suitable companions for such a community tank. However, *H. flammeus* is also quite compatible with virtually all other species mentioned in this book.

Hyphessobrycon bentosi—Ornate Tetra (formerly *H. ornatus*)

This is one of the most beautiful tetras. Adult males have an extended, sickle-shaped dorsal fin, but even the somewhat smaller female (fuller body and rounded dorsal fin) is still an attraction for any community tank, particularly when displayed against a dark bottom. The maximum size of *H. bentosi* is about 2½ inches.

H. bentosi is closely related to the blood tetras. It is frequently offered under the incorrect names of *H. serpae*, *H. rosaceus*, and *H. ornatus*. A school of ornate tetras is not overly active but instead moves sedately through the tank

Top: Often called the ornate tetra, *Hyphessobrycon bentosi* is closely related to the other serpae tetras but has much higher dorsal and anal fins. **Bottom:** Lemon tetras, *Hyphessobrycon pulchripinnis,* are just touched with a yellowish wash except for the front rays of the anal fin, which are often bright yellow.

or at times simply remains more or less stationary among water plants. Consequently, this fish should not be put together with hyperactive species. It is quite compatible with species that have the same maintenance requirements.

A varied diet is very important for proper growth and condition and should include live food such as mosquito larvae. With adequate care and attention *H. bentosi* may reach an age of five years in captivity.

Hyphessobrycon pulchripinnis — Lemon Tetra

°C

30
29
28
27
26
25
24
23
22
21
20
19

The lemon tetra is a native of the Amazon region, though its actual distribution is uncertain. It is assumed that it is found in the typical black waters of forest streams.

The lemon tetra is one of the more sedate members of this family, therefore it is important that there are adequate hiding places such as plant thickets as well as subdued lighting so that this fish can establish small territories. If a small tank is used, then the lemon tetra should not be kept together with fast-moving swimmers.

Lemon tetras provide nice color contrasts with red species such as any of the blood tetras or related forms. As far as food and feeding are concerned, lemon tetras are undemanding, feeding on virtually all foods. However, the diet should include supplements of live foods.

Maximum size is 2 inches, with males remaining slightly smaller than females. Color differences between the sexes are not obvious, though the black margin around the anal fin is extremely faint in females.

Top: A group of three male lemon tetras. Although not spectacular, they are attractive and have their supporters. **Bottom:** A male *Hyphessobrycon bentosi* in all its glory, the color bright and the fins spread.

°C

(South America: streams)

Hyphessobrycon erythrostigma — Bleeding Heart Tetra (formerly *H. rubrostigma*)

This species looks very similar to the previously discussed *H. bentosi* but is characterized by a blood-red round spot just above the abdominal cavity. It was introduced to the aquarium trade from Colombia toward the end of the 1950's. The maximum size is about 3¾ inches.

The bleeding heart tetra is peaceful and in behavior and maintenance requirements it is essentially indistinguishable from *H. bentosi*. As far as breeding is concerned this fish is considered to be a "problem fish."

Although there are already more than 1,000 species of tetras known from South America many of which are suitable for an aquarium, new attractively colored species are continuously imported. Usually these are members of the genera *Hemigrammus* and *Hyphessobrycon*. Tetras are also widely distributed throughout Africa; about 200 species are known so far. However, these are not nearly as popular as those from tropical and subtropical South America.

°C

Pristella maxillaris — Pristella (formerly *P. riddlei*)

This fish lives in dense underwater plant beds close to the banks in small tributaries of larger rivers in Brazil. Usually these are streams with very little water. The species ranges over much of northern South America.

The tank should be large and densely planted along the sides and back, with sufficient swimming space in the front and center. As a typical schooling fish, the pristella should

Top: Bleeding heart tetras, *Hyphessobrycon erythrostigma*, are among the most spectacular of tetras, the long, flowing fins and bright colors, including the red heart mark, putting them into a class to themselves. **Bottom:** Attractive but not especially colorful, the pristella, *Pristella maxillaris*, is easily kept and looks best in large schools.

always be kept in a large group of 10 to 20 fish rather than just two or three individuals, which may then be seen as pale little fish hiding among the plants. The maximum size is about 2 inches, with the males somewhat smaller than the females; females have a fuller abdomen. Breeding the pristella is generally not difficult, but not in a community tank. It is an omnivorous fish that should be given live foods on occasion. The water must be crystal clear and of good quality.

The pristella is a very peaceful fish that is ideally suited for any community tank. It goes well together with other tetras, especially neon tetras and head and tail lights, with a school of barbs, with livebearers, and with all bottom-dwellers. All these species have a preferred temperature range from 72-75 °F. Anyone interested in observing the schooling behavior of the pristella should keep as many possible together and if need be omit a couple of other species.

°C *(Africa; rivers)*

Phenacogrammus interruptus — Congo Tetra

```
30
29
28
27
26
25
24
23
22
21
20
19
```

One of the most spectacular sights for any aquarist is a school of Congo tetras cruising in a large, roomy tank against a dark background and dark bottom. If there are additionally a couple of dozen neon tetras among some cryptorynes slightly closer to the bottom and the surface is covered with some floating plants such as *Ceratopteris* to provide subdued lighting, this is such a pretty picture that no other fishes are required.

With such a combination of fishes it is important to observe the correct temperature requirements, because Congo tetras need slightly higher temperatures than neon

A pair of large adult Congo tetras in a well-planted tank is a spectacular sight. The streaming fins of the male when combined with the iridescence of the scales make this a truly unique fish.

tetras. However, both species should be contented at 75°F. Congo tetras can be somewhat shy and should not be placed together with active swimmers.

P. interruptus comes from the Congo River and its tributaries. Males have veil-like extended fins and can reach a maximum size of 4 to 5 inches   while the females remain smaller (3¼ inches). Juvenile males can be recognized very early by the white margin of the anal fin.

One of the undesirable traits of this fish is that it eats too much! Therefore, food should be given in moderation, but the diet must be varied and include live foods. This fish likes to catch insects and larvae from near the surface; mealworms are also taken (do not give too much of these), as are water fleas; give dried foods only as a supplement.

Family Cyprinidae

°C

| 30 |
| 29 |
| 28 |
| 27 |
| 26 |
| 25 |
| 24 |
| 23 |
| 22 |
| 21 |
| 20 |
| 19 |

(Southeast Asia; small rivers)
Tanichthys albonubes — **White Cloud Mountain Minnow**

This species was discovered by either a Chinese scoutmaster or a little Chinese boy, but either way soon became an important aquarium fish. It is now difficult to collect in the White Cloud mountains of Canton, China, and it is far easier to breed the fish in hatcheries in Hong Kong. Males are slightly more slender and have more intense colors than females. Maximum size is about 1½ inches.

Top: The Congo tetra, *Phenacogrammus interruptus*, is one of the larger tetras, but it is shy and does not do well with fast-moving fishes. **Bottom:** The White Cloud, *Tanichthys albonubes*, is one of the few common aquarium fishes that originated in mainland China. Several distinctive color varieties and fin varieties are bred.

84

It is hardy fish that can be kept in an unheated tank at room temperature (about 68°F). It goes well together with rosy barbs, bloodfins, guppies, zebras, and corydoras catfishes. At a temperature of about 72°F (never in excess of 75°F) the White Cloud Mountain minnow can be kept with tetras that prefer cooler water.

This is an active fish that requires a fair amount of swimming space. The tank—preferably long—must be planted only along the sides and back with plants like *Myriophyllum*. Although this is primarily a mid-water species, at times it will go down to the bottom in search of food. Since virtually all of the suitable inhabitants of a community tank with the White Cloud have similar behavior patterns, there must be a few "sandy patches" among the bottom gravel for them to "dig" in. It is important for the well-being of this species that it is kept only as small schools. Food is no problem, as *T. albonubes* will feed on all sorts of things. Live foods are definitely preferred. Tubifex worms should be chopped into small pieces.

MID-WATER FISHES, DENSELY PLANTED
Family Anabantidae

(Southeast Asia: densely overgrown waters)

Colisa fasciata — Giant Gourami, Banded Gourami

This fish is a native of the lowlands of northern and eastern India, Bangladesh, Burma, Thailand, and Malaysia. It is often mistaken for the rarely imported thick-lipped gourami, *C. labiosa*. When introduced into a tank it may initially be shy, but when settled in the fish becomes active, sometimes even slightly aggressive. It likes to hide among *Limnophila, Cryptocoryne*, and underneath floating plants such as water sprite.

°C

30
29
28
27
26
25
24
23
22
21
20
19

Two colorful gouramis. **Top:** *Colisa fasciata,* the giant gourami; **bottom:** *Colisa lalia,* the dwarf gourami. The dwarf gourami is kept more often than the giant, as the colors of breeding males have to be seen to be believed.

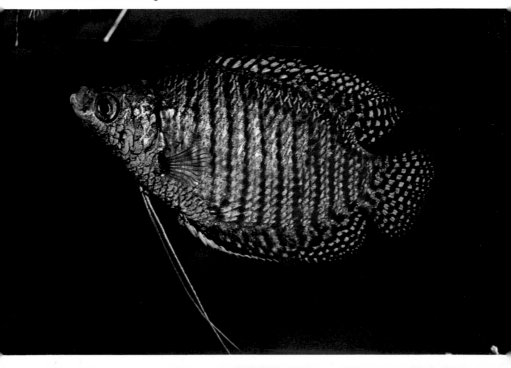

The maximum size of *C. fasciata* is about 5 inches. It requires a varied diet, although all commercially available fish foods are eagerly taken.

It is unlikely that males will build a bubblenest in a community tank. This fish is also attractive as a member of the "Southeast Asian tank," together with other species from that area. Such a community tank could contain two pairs each of *C. fasciata, Trichogaster leeri,* and *Colisa lalia,* as well as at least a dozen *Rasbora heteromorpha.* This is essentially a fish community as it could be encountered in the wild. The bottom of such a tank could be stocked with kuhli loaches. A large submerged tree root (well-soaked) would be very attractive in such a tank.

Colisa lalia — Dwarf Gourami

This is a very close relative of the banded gourami. It is found throughout the lowlands of large Indian river systems such as the Brahmaputra and the Ganges. There it inhabits the flood plains, primarily in shallow, standing bodies of water of all kinds.

Compared to *C. fasciata,* the dwarf gourami shows little variation in color and size. In fact, maximum size of this cute little fish is about 2 inches. When first placed into a tank the dwarf gourami tends to be a bit shy, but after a little while it usually settles in quite nicely. Males are very conspicuous with their brighter, more intense coloration. In females the rows of dots against the brownish background are less obvious.

In addition to their well-developed gills, labyrinth fishes (gouramis, bettas) also possess an additional respiratory

°C

30
29
28
27
26
25
24
23
22
21
20
19

A spawning male dwarf gourami, *Colisa lalia,* is a stunning sight. In the right light the blue and orange colors shine with a life all their own.

organ, the labyrinth, under the gill covers. This enables them to breathe air, which is very important in oxygen-depleted waters where these fishes often occur. Although incredibly high temperatures have been recorded in some of the native labyrinth fish habitats, this does not mean similar conditions must prevail in a community tank setting. Despite the fact that these fishes can adapt to extreme conditions, they do better and live longer at temperatures below 86°F and within a normal dissolved oxygen range. Labyrinth fishes are essentially omnivores, feeding on all commercially available tropical fish foods. However, the diet should include some live foods and some plant material.

Tanks for labyrinth fishes must have a low water level (about 8 inches) and a secure cover. The warm air that accumulates between the cover and the water's surface prevents the fish from catching a "cold" when they come up to the surface to breathe. Floating plants must not cover the entire surface: be sure to leave sufficient open space for these fish to breathe.

°C

30

29

28

27

26

25

24

23

22

21

20

19

Trichogaster leeri — Pearl Gourami, Mosaic Gourami

The pearl gourami is found in rivers of the lowlands and highlands of Thailand, Malaysia, and Indonesia (Sumatra and Borneo). It prefers shallow, densely overgrown waters and is rarely ever seen in open water. In an aquarium it tends to be shy if there is insufficient plant cover around.

In spite of its considerable size (maximum 5 inches), the pearl gourami can be placed with even the smallest fish. It is a peaceful fish that does not like to be bothered by extremely active swimmers around it. *Colisa* species or some

Top: A pair of pearl gouramis, *Trichogaster leeri*. This large species is extremely peaceful and colorful but has a reputation for delicacy. **Bottom:** The blue or three-spot gourami, *Trichogaster trichopterus,* is the most common gourami in the hobby and comes in many different color varieties.

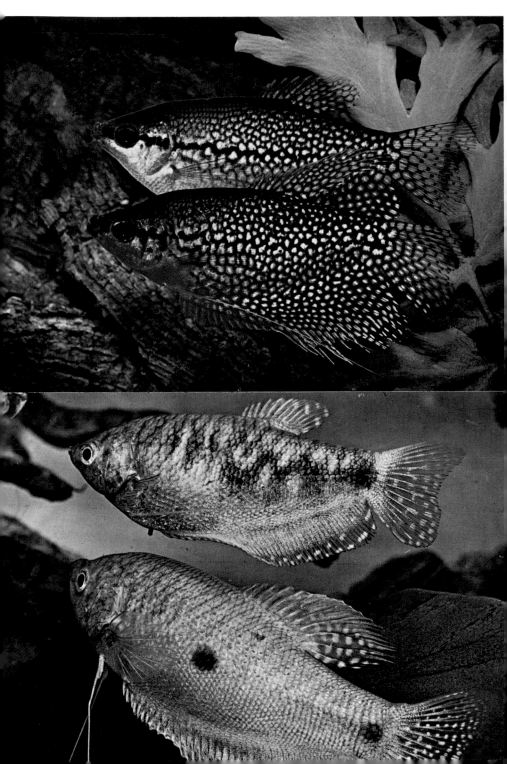

rasboras are good company. If the community tank is sufficiently large and properly set up so that each species can establish some sort of territory, it may even be possible to add other species such as South American tetras, especially *Hemigrammus ocellifer.*

Plants have to be selected according to their ability to tolerate high temperatures (*e.g., Limnophila, Ceratopteris, Hygrophila, Cryptocoryne*). It is important to have a cover of floating plants as a light filter. The bottom can be covered with fine-grained gravel, and a decorative piece of tree root (well-soaked!) gives some character to the underwater landscape.

The water level must be kept relatively low (about 8 inches). If pearl gouramis are to be kept together with species that are active swimmers, the tank size has to be selected accordingly. That is, the tank must be sufficiently long rather than high and wide. A pair of angelfish (*Pterophyllum*)— which would require a high tank—would be totally out of place in such a low and long tank. Tiger barbs have a tendency to "nibble" on the thread-like fins of pearl gouramis and thus should be kept away. Some other barb species make good company for pearl gouramis.

Females are less intensely colored than males; moreover, their dorsal fin is rounded off rather than extended as in males. The courtship coloration of males is quite spectacular. Pearl gouramis are omnivorous feeders, but their diet should contain some vegetable matter.

Trichogaster trichopterus—Blue Gourami, Three-spot Gourami

The blue variety of this species is far more popular

The numerous filaments on the fins of this fish, plus of course the orange breast, mark it as a spawning male pearl gourami. Notice the very elongate ventral fins, also a characteristic of male gouramis.

°C
30
29
28
27
26
25
24
23
22
21
20
19

among aquarists than the orginal form, which is native to Southeast Asia and Indonesia. Care and maintenance are the same as for *T. leeri.*

These fish often live under extremely poor conditions in their native habitats in over-heated drainage ditches, polluted ponds, and sun-burned rice paddies. In clean water with normal temperatures these fish tend to do much better, as can readily be seen from their more attractive coloration and their behavior.

Trichogaster and *Colisa* species are often referred to in German as "thread-finned fishes" because of the thread-like extensions of their pelvic fins. These highly movable "threads" or filaments are equipped with sense buds that enable the fish to find their way through dense plant thickets.

(Southeast Asia: plankton-rich waters)
Helostoma temmincki — Kissing Gourami

°C
30
29
28
27
26
25
24
23
22
21
20
19

Because of their peculiar "kissing" habit (a species-specific behavior pattern that consists of biting at each other's jaw and tugging), kissing gouramis are very popular fish for community tanks. The aquarium must have some algal growth if this fish is to do well, however.

In their natural habitat (rice paddies of Thailand, Malaysia, and Indonesia) this fish can get quite large, but in an aquarium it will remain suitably small. It is peaceful and undemanding and virtually feeds itself by keeping the algae in check. With its thick, finely folded lips this fish rasps algae off plant leaves, the glass, rocks, etc. However, it should also receive some supplementary feeding in the form of fine dried and live foods.

Top: Kissing gouramis, *Helostoma temmincki,* are valued more for their odd "kissing" behavior than for their colors, which are usually quite plain. A green variety also is common. **Bottom:** The angelfish, *Pterophyllum scalare,* is a stately beauty greatly desired by all beginning hobbyists.

94

In aquarium circles a pinkish color mutant is more common than the greenish gray wild form. The sexes can only be distinguished when they approach maturity; the females are slightly heavier in build than males.

A community tank for *H. temmincki* should be planted with *Limnophila, Cryptocoryne,* and *Hygrophila;* part of the surface should be covered with floating plants.

This peaceful fish is compatible with nearly all species listed in this book.

Family Cichlidae

(South America: along river banks)
Pterophyllum scalare — Angelfish, Scalare

The angelfish is instantly recognizable by its highly arched back (maximum length 6 inches, maximum body height 7 to 10 inches) and long fins. Because of its shape it prefers to move through reed beds and plant thickets rather than swim in open water. Originally this fish was collected in the Guyanas and northern Brazil (especially the Rio Negro, middle reaches of the Amazon, and Rio Tapajoz) and shipped to Europe and North America. Nowadays it is hatchery-raised on a commercial scale.

The majestic angelfish varies greatly in form and color. The marbled angelfish and the fancy-finned varieties are very popular with aquarists. Angelfish are basically carnivorous, so they should be given adequate live or fresh-frozen foods. Sometimes they will also take dried foods, but this should always be supplemented with live foods.

Angelfish do best in large, relatively high tanks planted heavily with *Cryptocoryne,* giant *Vallisneria, Echinodorus, Sagittaria,* and *Cabomba,* which provide adequate cover. Reed thickets can be simulated with thin bamboo sticks (caution: these must not be chemically treated for use in

°C

30
29
28
27
26
25
24
23
22
21
20
19

gardens or plant nurseries). A small group of angelfish will establish their own territories and will leave the other fishes in peace. They should not be put together with fast-swimming fishes, which tend to upset them. The "mood" of each angelfish can easily be gauged (as for most cichlids) by the intensity of their colors, particularly the black vertical bands. Males and females are hard to distinguish outside the breeding season.

The most suitable companions for angelfish are some of the larger tetras (NOT neon tetras!). The bottom of the tank can be stocked with dwarf cichlids or with catfishes. Livebearers can occupy the niche close to the surface. It is important to select suitable tank dimensions for such a community tank; a tank should have a minimum height of at least 16 inches, the same width, and a length of about 48 inches.

Modern tank-raised angelfish are easy to keep and even breed well, but their long fins serve as bait for barbs and similar fishes if they are kept in the community aquarium.

SCHOOLING FISHES OF UPPER WATERS
Family Gasteropelecidae

(South America: shallow waters)
Gasteropelecus sternicla — **Silver Hatchetfish**

This widely distributed South American hatchetfish can actually "fly" with strokes of its powerful, wing-like pectoral fins. Observations vary, but the observed flights seem to range from barely 6 feet to about 12 feet. However, in an aquarium this fish cannot fly but only jumps. Therefore, the tank has to be roomy, especially long, wide, and *must be tightly covered!*

Hatchetfishes are native to much of northern and central South America. There they occur primarily in shallow regions of slowly flowing or standing jungle water, in rivers, streams, ponds, and swamps.

°C
30
29
28
27
26
25
24
23
22
21
20
19

Top: The silver hatchetfish, *Gasteropelecus sternicla,* is one of several similar hatchetfish species often imported. They almost always must have live foods.
Bottom: Boehlke's penquin or hockeystick, *Thayeria boehlkei,* is distinctive in both color pattern and oblique swimming position.

As do most other surface-swimmers, hatchetfishes feed primarily on flying insects and their larvae that fall into the water. Sometimes they will also take dried foods but they are especially fond of mosquito larvae. Any tank with hatchetfishes should be filled to only two-thirds of its height or preferably even less and should contain only species that are equally as peaceful as *G. sternicla*. The silver hatchetfish reaches a maximum size just under 3 inches. The middle and lower zones of the tank can be filled with tetras and bottom-fishes. A dense plant cover along the sides and back is desirable, as well as leafy floating plants (be sure to leave some open areas on the surface). A few well-soaked pieces of root in a dark bottom always looks very attractive.

Little is known about sexual differences and the reproductive biology of this hatchetfish, which was imported for the aquarium trade as early as 1912.

°C

30
29
28
27
26
24
23
22
21
20
19

(South America; slowly flowing waters)
Thayeria boehlkei — Boehlke's Penguin

The broad black stripe running into the lower lobe of the tail and the oblique (tail down) swimming position set this species very much apart from most other tetras. A school of penguins provides an attractive counterpoint to a school of glowlight tetras or blood tetras in the same tank. The fact that this fish remains close to the surface clearly demonstrates that in the wild flying insects dropping onto the water make up a significant amount of the diet. Thus, small insects (fruitflies) must be included in the diet. It will feed on almost any fish foods, but preferably at the surface.

In *Thayeria boehlkei* the black lateral stripe runs along midbody to just behind the head **(top)**, while in the similar *Thayeria obliqua* **(bottom)**, also often imported, the black lateral stripe runs upward and fades under the dorsal fin.

The tank must be long to provide adequate swimming space as well as have sufficient hiding places among the plants. A partial cover of floating plants is recommended. These fish have a tendency to jump, therefore the tank must have a tight-fitting cover. Maximum size is over 3 inches.

T. boehlkei is a native of Peru (Rio Maranon) and the upper Amazon. Males are slightly more slender than females. Suitable companions are a pair of bottom-dwelling dwarf cichlids. Angelfish, *Pterophyllum*, which can move about among the plants, can be compatible with *Thayeria* provided the tank is sufficiently high for the *Pterophyllum* and has sufficient swimming space for this tetra.

Family Cyprinidae

°C

(Southeast Asia: open water)
Brachydanio albolineatus — Pearl Danio

30
29
28
27
26
25
24
23
22
21
20
19

This active, agile swimmer comes from rivers and streams (even ponds, lakes, and rice paddies) in Burma, Thailand, Malaysia, and Sumatra. In its native habitat the pearl danio reaches a maximum size of about 2¼ inches, but these days hatchery-bred specimens rarely ever reach that size. Also, wild-caught fish (imported for the first time in 1911) are alleged to be far more beautiful than captive progeny. There is also a yellow color mutant (the gold danio) in the aquarium fish trade, yet the wild form is far more attractive in a community tank. Males are more slender and more strongly colored than females.

Top: The pearl danio, *Brachydanio albolineatus,* is a study in muted colors but makes an attractive school. **Bottom:** *Brachydanio frankei,* the leopard danio, is often considered a hybrid or a mutation of the zebra danio, but it is certainly distinct in pattern.

102

Pearl danios are not particularly choosy when it comes to food; they prefer to feed from the surface but will also pick up food from the bottom without digging for it. The diet should be diversified. Dried food is eagerly taken but should be supplemented with small live foods at times.

A long, bright tank with plenty of swimming room and moderately dense planting with *Vallisneria, Elodea, Ludwigia, Vesicularia, Cryptocorynes, Limnophila, Nitella, Cabomba,* or *Myriophyllum* is ideal for all *Brachydanio* species. However, as active swimmers all of them have a tendency to jump, thus a tight-fitting tank cover is mandatory.

The bottom can be covered with coarse gravel, and a few larger stones and a decorative submerged (well-soaked) tree root can look very attractive in such a community tank. Although in nature pearl danios and harlequin rasboras are alleged to occur together, they should not be kept together in a community tank. The colors of *B. albolineatus* are most spectacular under top lighting, while harlequins look most attractive under subdued lighting in a densely planted tank with a dark bottom.

On the other hand, a school of silver-tipped tetras (*Hasemania nana)* or flame tetras (*Hyphessobrycon flammeus*) goes very well with pearl danios. Such a tank is always full of activity and life. The fishes will chase each other in never-ending playfulness – they never seem to get tired.

Brachydanio frankei — Leopard Danio

The only thing known about the history of the leopard danio, which resembles the zebra danio in shape and is perhaps a mutation or hybrid, is that it was first noticed in a

°C
30
29
28
27
26
25
24
22
21
20
19

Top: Danios often hybridize. Shown are hybrids between the zebra and pearl danios. **Bottom:** Male pearl danios are much more slender than the females, which are often swollen with eggs.

104

tropical fish hatchery in Prague in 1961. It is not identical with any of the other known *Brachydanio* species. It is such an attractive fish that it rapidly became popular outside of Czechoslovakia, where it became a real sensation among aquarists.

The maximum size is about 1¾ inches, although some aquarists insist that it grows to 2½ inches. Care and requirements are the same as for all other *Brachydanio* species. This fish sometimes has a unexplained tendency to lose condition for no apparent reason.

In a community tank *B. frankei* goes well with a school of White Cloud Mountain minnows or a school of South American tetras. However, since *Brachydanios* like bright tanks, it is not advisable to put them together with "glowing" tetras such as neons or cardinals because these are more effectively displayed under subdued lighting and against a dark bottom. The zone close to the bottom is ideally filled with a school of rosy barbs.

°C

30
29
28
27
26
25
24
23
22
21
20
19

(Southeast Asia: standing water)
Brachydanio nigrofasciatus — Spotted Danio

The literature indicates Burma to be the place where this species was originally collected, but one can assume it is also found in standing and flowing waters in the adjacent countries. A school of spotted danios appears to be somewhat less active than the other danios described above. Nevertheless, *B. nigrofasciatus* looks attractive in any community tank, and it is indeed compatible with most if not all species listed in this book.

Top: The spotted danio, *Brachydanio nigrofasciatus,* looks rather like a plain zebra danio and behaves much like one also. **Bottom:** The zebra danio, *Brachydanio rerio,* is often one of the first egg-layers bred by beginning hobbyists.

The maximum size is about 1¾ inches. Adult females have fuller bodies than the more slender males. Care and maintenance are easy: all that is needed is a long tank and a nutritious balanced diet.

Brachydanio rerio — Zebra Danio, Striped Danio

Older aquarists often complain that inbreeding and mass production of this fish (imported for the first time in 1905) have reduced its appearance to "a mere shadow of its former self." Nevertheless, it is still equally popular with beginning as well as with advanced aquarists. While *B. rerio* was initially as expensive as most marine fishes are today, it is now one of the cheapest tropical fishes.

This beautiful and peaceful little fish from eastern India reaches a maximum size of 2 inches, is quite hardy, and can be bred easily in captivity, but not in a community tank. Aquarists are advised to keep a small spare tank ready and try their hand at breeding *B. rerio*. The adult female can be distinguished from the male by her plumper body. A pair is introduced into a shallow tank with a water temperature of at least 77°F. The bottom should be covered with bushy plants or with a spawning grill. Spawning usually takes place during the early morning hours. The pair must be removed immediately once spawning has been completed because the parents will try to feed on their own eggs. The young can be reared with extremely small foods (both dried and live).

A community tank featuring zebras should be as long and shallow as possible because this fish is an extremely active and fast swimmer. It prefers lighted areas and moves

°C

30
29
28
27
26
25
24
23
22
21
20
19

Recently the zebra danio has been developed into an aquarium variety with long, flowing fins. This variety is avidly sought by many hobbyists.

108

through all water zones; however, the surface is often pre-ferred. The tank must have a tight-fitting cover since *B. rerio* tends to jump.

As a typical omnivorous feeder, the zebra will accept all sorts of food. Maximum age in captivity seems to be about three years. Fairly low temperatures are tolerated, so the zebra danio can be kept in outdoor ponds during the warm summer months. There they would go well together with rosy barbs and White Cloud Mountain minnows. In a community tank setting, *B. rerio* goes well with South American tetras and also with most of the species mentioned in this book, with the exception of those preferring subdued lighting.

(Southeast Asia: standing and flowing waters)
Rasbora dorsiocellata — Hi-spot **Rasbora**

°C

30
29
28
27
26
25
24
23
22
21
20
19

This delicate-appearing rasbora occurs in Thailand, Malaysia, and Sumatra. It is a peaceful, active, and hardy aquarium fish. The maximum size is about 1½ inches. Rasboras are very fond of small live foods, although all commercial foods of small enough size are taken.

Adult females can be distinguished from males by their fuller bodies and more yellowish tails (in the male the tail invariably has a reddish tinge). This fish looks most effective under subdued lighting, which is best provided through a cover of floating plants. The bottom can have a thin layer of well-soaked peat moss. In order to maintain maximum swimming space, such a tank is planted only along the sides and back.

Top: The little hi-spot rasbora, *Rasbora dorsiocellata,* is surprisingly hardy and easy to maintain, especially if small live foods are available. **Bottom:** The broad black wedge-shaped mark on the posterior sides of the common or harlequin rasbora, *Rasbora heteromorpha,* is distinctive although somewhat variable.

110

Hi-spot rasboras can be kept in a community tank together with other East Asian fishes or with South American or African fishes.

(Southeast Asia: small standing waters)
Rasbora heteromorpha — Rasbora, Harlequin Fish

This pinkish red fish excited fish collectors, scientists, and aquarists alike when it was first imported into Europe in 1906; it caused nearly as much excitement as the later importation of neon tetras. However, it took a long time to discover the breeding secret of the rasbora, so for years it had to be imported primarily from Chinese dealers to cover the enormous demand for this fish from aquarists. Since then it has been discovered that the reproductive behavior of *R. heteromorpha* differs significantly from that of its closest relatives, and now large tropical fish hatcheries produce virtually the entire commercial demand.

°C

30
29
28
27
26
25
24
23
22
21
20
19

In contrast to the other rasboras that cast their eggs randomly into the water, *R. heteromorpha* attaches its eggs to water plants. Since the captive progeny of this fish have now become much hardier than the orginally imported (disease suceptible) fish, they can be kept in normal tap water without difficulty, provided the water is not too hard. However, breeding still requires soft water.

Males and females can be distinguished by the outline of the wedge-shaped black mark: in males the lower tip of this mark is drawn out and extended further downward than in females. Moreover, the male has a slightly smaller, more slender body with brighter coloration. These sexual differences require some expertise to be useful consistently.

The common rasbora differs from most other rasbora species not only in color pattern but also in breeding behavior. It is the only commonly seen rasbora that lays its eggs attached to a large leaf. This fish must be kept in schools to be effective.

112

The maximum size is about 1¾ inches. In their native habitat these fish inhabit flood plains overgrown with aquatic plants, ditches, and creeks; frequently these are little more than small water puddles. The harlequin is an omnivorous feeder, accepting all sorts of foods with a preference for small live foods picked up off the surface.

The bottom should be dark, possibly covered with a *thin* layer of peat moss, to bring out the best colors in the rasbora. Other substances that contain tannic acid, which gives a "tea color" appearance to the water, can also be used. The most suitable plants are *Cryptocoryne*, *Limnophila*, *Synnema*, *Ceratopteris*, and *Hygrophila*.

When keeping rasboras together with South American tetras it is important to keep an eye on the temperature requirements; regrettably, rasboras are often kept far too cool!

(Southeast Asia: flood plains)
Rasbora trilineata — Three-Lined or Scissortailed Rasbora

°C
30
29
28
27
26
25
24
23
22
21
20
19

Scissortailed rasboras occur in Thailand, Malaysia, and on some of the Indonesian islands. In the wild they reach a maximum size of about 6 inches, but in an aquarium they reach only about 3 inches. They are peaceful, active, and easily fed (they are particularly fond of mosquito larvae), all essential assets for a good community tank fish. The tank should be as large as possible and preferably fairly long. Since this is fast-swimming fish that tends to jump, the tank must be equipped with a tight-fitting cover.

Scissortailed rasboras have a characteristically marked tail fin that together with the metallic gray of the body provides a nice contrast to brightly colored fishes such as *Brachydanio* species. It is also quite compatible with tetras and livebearers. The bottom of such a community tank can be stocked with any other species.

114

Although there are numerous described *Rasbora* species, new ones continue to be described. Among these newly found species are *Rasbora axelrodi* **(top)** and *Rasbora brittani* **(bottom)**, both described in the pages of *Tropical Fish Hobbyist* magazine.

LIVEBEARERS OF
THE UPPER WATERS

Family Poeciliidae

°C

30
29
28
27
26
25
24
23
22
21
20
19

(South America: standing waters)
Poecilia reticulata — Guppy (formerly *Lebistes reticulatus*)

Although the guppy is a hardy fish that can survive at least for a while at fairly low temperatures with an inadequate diet and the presence of incompatible aquarium companions, proper care and attention will very much improve its condition and appearance. This implies a nutritious, varied diet of dried food combined with vegetable matter and live food, proper swimming space, and a water temperature above 68°F. After all, the guppy is a native of the coastal tropics, such as Venezuela, Trinidad, Guyana, and

Top: *Rasbora trilineata,* the three-lined or scissortailed rasbora, is one of the larger species. Although not very colorful, they are peaceful. **Bottom:** The guppy, *Poecilia reticulata,* perhaps the best-known tropical fish.

northern Brazil. It was first discovered by Reverend Guppy in 1859 and in just a few decades had been introduced into many other tropical and subtropical countries to eradicate mosquitos. It now occurs over such a wide range that its original range is almost no longer recognizable.

The guppy was first introduced to Europe and the aquarium fish trade in 1908. Since then a number of different and often very colorful varieties have been bred. The guppy has a natural tendency—even in nature—to show strange variations in color and finnage; this is particularly true of males—no two males are ever alike. Guppy experts who have a sound knowledge of fish genetics have managed to breed some fantastic veil-tailed guppies that are now judged at tropical fish shows according to international standards.

In a well-planted tank with *Elodea, Myriophyllum, Vallisneria, Riccia, Cabomba, Sagittaria,* or *Ludwigia,* some of the new-born young will survive even in a community tank. The comparatively inconspicuously colored females grow to twice the size of males (maximum size for males is about 1¼ inches). The black "gravid spot" is typical of females ready to give birth.

The peaceful guppy fits into any community tank. Beginning aquarists should start out with a tank holding some of the other livebearers together with guppies. Some of the special strains are not suitable for a community tank.

(Central America: densely overgrown waters)
Poecilia velifera — Yucatan Sail-fin Molly (formerly *Mollienesia velifera*)

Anyone wishing to display this fish should make an effort to find really exquisite specimens. Unfortunately, shops often sell fish that bear little resemblance to an ideal Yucatan sail-fin molly. This species was discovered in eastern Mexico (the Yucatan Peninsula), where it inhabits quietly flowing waters with dense plant growth. Since it breeds readily in captivity it soon became one of the most popular aquarium fishes. Yucatan sail-fin mollies are active, relatively large fish (maximum size about 5 inches) that are best kept in the company of other livebearers such as guppies and swordtails. If the tank is densely planted some of the young born in the tank will grow up.

Sexual differences in body form can be seen only in mature animals. Males are characterized by the "sail-like" dorsal fin and a black margin along the outer edge of the tail. Like all familiar livebearers, the males have the anal fin modified as a gonopodium; the gonopodium is distinguishable when the fish is still very young.

Plants most suitable for a community tank featuring sail-fin mollies are *Cryptocoryne, Vallisneria,* and *Elodea;* some floating plants should also be present.

While a tank of just livebearers can contain slightly brackish water (about 3½ ounces of non-iodized salt per 2½ gallons) since they are found primarily in slightly salty coastal waters or hard interior drainages, if kept together with other species the addition of salt has to be omitted. Moreover, retiring, quiet species should not be kept together with sail-fin mollies, but *Brachydanios,* rainbowfishes, and corydoras catfishes are ideally suited as company for sail-fins.

It is of paramount importance that sail-fin mollies only be kept in a tank that has substantial algal growth. These fish require a strong plant component in their diet if they are to grow properly. They are also active jumpers, so the tank has to be securely covered.

The common sail-fin molly shipped from Florida fish farms is *Poecilia latipinna* of the southern United States. In many ways it is just like a smaller (3-4 inches) version of the Yucatan sail-fin and can be kept in much the same fashion. In the United States *Poecilia velifera* is seldom available for sale in pure form—all the common mollies have been hybridized.

°C

30
29
28
27
26
25
24
23
22
21
20
19

119

In the United States very few sail-finned mollies are sold except the native *Poecilia latipinna*. Because this species is common in much of Florida and readily establishes itself in the commercial ponds of fish farmers, it is often harvested as a side crop to typical tropical fishes. Large males raised under the best of water conditions and fed ample amounts of vegetable food have a stunning appearance.

Poecilia sp.—Black Molly

The black molly is the product of captive breeding, and its original form can no longer be traced with certainty. Therefore, it may be appropriate to describe this fish as a hybrid. It could possibly be a black variety of *Poecilia sphenops* or *Poecilia mexicana*, but some specimens are almost certainly crosses between one of these two *Poecilia* species and *P. latipinna*. Livebearers in general hybridize easily with closely related species and thus have a tendency to vary considerably in coloration and finnage.

There are pied forms as well as completely black fish. This characteristic of great color variation has endeared them to the hearts of professional breeders. Deliberate and painstaking breeding attempts in Southeast Asia have produced veil-tailed varieties that also have greatly lengthened anal, pelvic, and pectoral fins. Unfortunately, the most attractive varieties are no longer as robust as the original form.

Maximum size is about 3-4 inches. Black mollies are somewhat susceptible to diseases, and large temperature variations must be avoided at all costs. Similarly, black mollies should be kept only with those species that also re-

°C

30
29
28
27
26
25
24
23
22
21
20
19

Top: The Yucatan sail-fin molly, *Poecilia velifera*. Males with well-developed dorsal fins are highly prized by enthusiasts. **Bottom:** A black molly, *Poecilia* sp. Because of the confused history of black mollies and the possibility that they originated from several species, they cannot be given a meaningful scientific name.

quire elevated temperatures. The water has to be very clear. If kept under appropriate conditions, black mollies are excellent community tank fish. Their velvety black coloration forms a beautiful contrast to brightly colored African, South American, or Southeast Asian species.

Xiphophorus helleri — Swordtail

The swordtail, originally from the eastern coast of southern Mexico, Guatemala, Honduras, and Belize, has given rise to a number of highly attractive varieties through mutations and systematic inbreeding. Males have a gonopodium (an anal fin where the first few rays have become modified into a copulatory organ) and a "sword," which is essentially an extension of the lower fin rays of the tail. Pregnant females in most color patterns can be recognized by a characteristic dark "gravid spot" just in front of the anal fin and by the full abdomen, in addition to lacking the sword and gonopodium. Generally, females have a plumper, slightly more arched body (maximum size almost 5 inches) than the smaller males (maximum size about 3¼ inches excluding the sword).

Swordtails are active fish that should always be kept in groups and never alone. They need adequate swimming room and plant thickets for hiding. Swordtails will breed readily in a community if there is sufficient plant cover, including floating plants (*Ceratopteris, Riccia*), for the young to hide in until they are large enough to be safe. Since

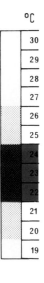

°C
30
29
28
27
26
25
24
23
22
21
20
19

Two types of swordtails, *Xiphophorus helleri*. At the top is a blue sword with normal fins; unfortunately the sword cannot be seen. At the bottom is a red Simpson high-finned swordtail male. Swordtails, guppies, and platies are among the most variable of fishes, especially when all the dozens of aquarium varieties are considered.

swordtails and platies of all types will hybridize easily, keeping a number of different forms together will result in mixing of the varieties.

Swordtails are definitely omnivorous, and they like to take their food from the surface (the mouth is especially adapted for surface feeding). Although they will grow on a diet of exclusively dried food, they will show better condition and color with a varied diet that includes vegetable matter and live foods.

The phenomenon of alleged sex changes among swordtails—females changing into males—has now been resolved. Apparently such fish have been males all along but reached their sexual maturity somewhat late. Although their body shape is reminiscent of females, after 12 to 18 months they suddenly develop a sword and a gonopodium within a few weeks. They will then also start to breed.

Males may reach sexual maturity at an age as early as 4½ months, but this type of male remains smaller and retains a straighter dorsal profile. It has been shown experimentally that there are two genetically rather different types among swordtail males. Such differentiation is determined by genetic factors. The progeny of "early" males contains conspicuously many more males, while that of "late" males has a majority of females. Sexually immature "late" males are often mistaken for females.

°C

30
29
28
27
26
25
21
20
19

Xiphophorus helleri X *Xiphophorus maculatus* — Red Simpson Swordtail

This spectacular variety with an incredibly large dorsal fin is a cross between green swordtails and platies. It was named in honor of its breeder, Mrs. Thelma Simpson. Many similar high-finned varieties have now been produced and are common.

Xiphophorus maculatus — Platy

°C

This species occurs naturally in a variety of different colors. It is a native of the shore regions of lakes, streams, and other slow-flowing waters in Mexico, Honduras, and Guatemala. Red, black, and pied variants were developed into pure forms by enthusiastic breeders. The wagtail platy, for instance, has a red body and black fins. The most popular form is the red platy, sometimes also called the coral platy. The maximum size for females is 2½ inches (males reach only 1¾ inches). These brightly colored fish will give a splash of color to any community tank. It is a peaceful, robust species that will feed on all sorts of foods and must have some vegetable matter. It also likes to feed on algae. It is important to never keep platies alone, but always in small groups.

Males do not have a sword, but instead have a rounded tail just as in females. The only external difference is the anal fin modified into a copulatory organ (gonopodium). Pregnant females can be recognized by the blackish "gravid spot."

Platies are closely related to swordtails and will hybridize, so new forms continually appear on the market. However, not all are fertile. Most commercially available platies certainly have swordtails among their ancestors. The comparatively inconspicuous wild forms usually are kept only in experimental laboratories and by geneticists.

Xiphophorus variatus — Sunset Platy, Platy Variatus

This platy is slightly larger than the common platy (females almost 3 inches, males 2 inches), but all other details regarding their care are identical. This species also has given rise to a great many different races, many being very colorful. Formerly platies had their own generic name — *Platypoecilus* — that is still widely used even though it has now become superceded. Platies are generally among the most ideal aquarium fish, and it is for this reason that much space has been devoted to them in this book. They are indeed the most suitable fish for beginning aquarists, who should always start out with livebearers. Moreover, a tank with livebearers always offers an opportunity to raise some of the young, provided there are enough plants to provide adequate cover and protection and one makes an effort to supply and feed the proper small food.

Generally speaking, even these undemanding livebearers require a steady, warm temperature, but occasional larger fluctuations are easily tolerated. This platy goes well with most other aquarium fishes, without regard to whether these are from Central or South America, from Southeast Asia, or from Africa. Only those species that could feel "harassed" by livebearers (*e.g.*, some labyrinth fishes) should be avoided in such a community tank.

The major disadvantage of the really high-finned swordtail varieties is that all the fins are elongated, including the gonopodium, the modified anal fin of the male. If the gonopodium is too long the fish cannot breed naturally, so females must be artificially inseminated, the gonopodium must be clipped to usable size, or the fish must be bred when very young before full finnage is developed.

The two aquarium platies. At the top is an all-red or blood platy, a form of *Xiphophorus maculatus*. At the bottom is a moderately colorful variety of the platy variatus, *Xiphophorus variatus*. Many platy varieties owe their existence to crosses of these two species and the swordtail.

INDEX

Acanthophthalmus kuhlii, 32, 34, 36
Acanthophthalmus myersi, 33
Acanthophthalmus semicinctus, 33, 36
Angelfish, 95-97
Aphyocharax anisitsi, 62, 63
Apistogramma borelli, 28-30
Australian dwarf rainbowfish, 44-46
Black molly, 120-122
Black ruby barb, 53-56
Black tetra, 66, 67
Bleeding heart tetra, 80, 81
Bloodfin, 62, 63
Blue gourami, 91, 92, 94
Botia macracantha, 36-39
Botia sidthimunki, 37, 38
Brachydanio albolineatus, 102-105
Brachydanio frankei, 103-106
Brachydanio nigrofasciatus, 106-108
Brachydanio rerio, 8, 107-110
Bronze corydoras, 16, 18, 19
Buenos Aires tetra, 68, 69
Callistus tetra, 72, 73
Capoeta oligolepis, 56-58
Capoeta schuberti, 57-59
Capoeta tetrazona, 59-61
Capoeta titteya, 61, 62
Cardinal tetra, 7, 49, 50, 51, 106
Checker barb, 56, 57
Checkerboard loach, 37, 38
Cherry barb, 61, 62
Chinese algae-eater, 41-43
Clown loach, 6, 36, 39
Colisa fasciata, 86-88
Colisa lalia, 87-90
Congo tetra, 82-84
Corydoras aeneus, 16, 19
Corydoras paleatus, 18, 19
Corydoras reticulatus, 17
Ctenobrycon spilurus, 63-65
Dwarf Egyptian mouthbrooder, 21-24
Dwarf gourami, 87-90
Flame tetra, 74, 75, 104
Gasteropelecus sternicla, 98, 100
Giant gourami, 86-88
Glossolepis incisus, 47
Glowlight tetra, 45-47
Golden dwarf cichlid, 30, 31
Guppy, 116-118
Gymnocorymbus ternetzi, 66, 67, 69
Gyrinocheilus aymonieri, 41-43
Half-banded loach, 33, 36
Half-striped barb, 57-59
Harlequin rasbora, 35, 36, 111-114
Hasemania nana, 70, 71, 104
Head-and-tail-light tetra, 70, 71
Helostoma temmincki, 94-96
Hemichromis bimaculatus, 27
Hemichromis thomasi, 25-27
Hemigrammus caudovittatus, 68, 69
Hemigrammus erythrozonus, 45-47
Hemigrammus ocellifer, 70-72, 92
Hi-spot rasbora, 110-112
High-finned dwarf cichlid, 28, 29

Hoplosternum thoracatum, 20, 21
Hyphessobrycon bentosi, 76-78
Hyphessobrycon callistus, 72, 73, 75
Hyphessobrycon erythrostigma, 80, 81
Hyphessobrycon flammeus, 74-76, 104
Hyphessobrycon pulchripinnis, 77-79
Kissing gourami, 94-96
Kribensis, 24, 25
Kuhli loach, 32-34
Labeo bicolor, 40-43
Lemon tetra, 77-79
Leopard danio, 103-106
Melanotaenia maccullochi, 44, 45
Nannacara anomala, 29-32
Neon tetra, 14, 15, 30, 48, 49, 97, 106
New Guinea red rainbowfish, 47
Ornate tetra, 76, 77
Paracheirodon axelrodi, 7, 49-51
Paracheirodon innesi, 15, 48-50
Pearl danio, 102-105
Pearl gourami, 90-93
Pelvicachromis pulcher, 24-26
Penguins, 48, 99-102
Peppered corydoras, 18, 19
Phenacogrammus interruptus, 82-85
Platy variatus, 9, 125-127
Poecilia latipinna, 120
Poecilia reticulata, 116-118
Poecilia sp., 120-122
Poecilia velifera, 118-121
Port Hoplo, 20-21
Pristella maxillaris, 80-82
Pseudocrenilabrus multicolor, 21-23
Pterophyllum scalare, 92, 95-97, 102
Puntius conchonius, 52, 55
Rasbora axelrodi, 115
Rasbora brittani, 115
Rasbora dorsiocellata, 30, 110-112
Rasbora heteromorpha, 34, 35, 88, 111-114
Rasbora trilineata, 114, 117
Red Simpson swordtail, 124
Red-tailed black shark, 40, 41, 43
Rosy barb, 52-54, 106, 110
Scissortailed rasbora, 114, 117
Silver hatchetfish, 98-100
Silver tetra, 63-65
Silver-tipped tetra, 70, 71, 104
Spotted danio, 106-108
Swordtail, 122-124
Tanichthys albonubes, 84-86
Thayeria boehlkei, 30, 48, 99-102
Thayeria obliqua, 101
Tiger barb, 36, 59-62
Trichogaster leeri, 88, 90-94
Trichogaster trichopterus, 91, 92, 94
White Cloud Mountain minnow, 24, 54,
  84-86, 106, 110
Xiphophorus helleri, 122-124
Xiphophorus helleri X *maculatus*, 124
Xiphophorus maculatus, 125, 127
Xiphophorus variatus, 9, 125-127
Yucatan sail-fin molly, 118-121
Zebra danio, 8, 107-110